SAFE
AND
SOUND

SAFE

AND

SOUND

Discovering Who You Really Are
Through Freedom In Christ

UNTIL CHRIST IS FORMED

BOOK ONE

Paul Anderson-Walsh

New Wine Press

New Wine Ministries
PO Box 17
Chichester
West Sussex
United Kingdom
PO19 2AW

ISBN 1-905991-40-2

Typeset by **documen**, www.documen.co.uk
Cover design by CCD, www.ccdgroup.co.uk
Printed in the United Kingdom

DEDICATION

To my precious children,

Chantelle, Louisa, Francesca and Paul

You've taught me the meaning of unconditional love
and acceptance and through my feeble attempts to be
a good father to you I've learnt most of what I know
about the Father of us all.

"(May you) become such as I am –
except for these chains."
(Acts 26:29)

ACKNOWLEDGEMENTS

My perpetual thanks to Hayley, my hero,
who continues to believe in the implausible.

Thank you too to the meticulous William Lee
who continues to help make sense of my English.

And my thanks to Tim Pettingale for
championing my cause as a writer.

FOREWORD

The Apostle Paul once said that we are each a work of divine art. "His workmanship created in Christ Jesus" is the way he described it. Embedded within the lines, colors and shadings of our lives is a beautiful picture. It is a marvelous work of grace.

The Divine Artist delights in displaying the beauty of His grace in human frames. Paul Anderson-Walsh displays the very message he teaches in a riveting manner. His is a picture of how a Loving Father can take the pigments of scared little orphans and create masterpieces of grace. He encourages us all to know that what God so wonderfully has done in him, He is doing in each of us.

Until Chist Is Formed is like a palette of an artist. With broad strokes that inspire and meticulous details that instruct, Paul shows us how the One who paints the sunset in the sky is, at this very moment, producing an even greater masterpiece on the canvas of our lives. The work of the Divine Artist will not stop in you until Christ *is* formed so that you display His image clearly.

This book will inspire and encourage you. It will indeed cause you to feel safe and sound. Don't be surprised if you find yourself experiencing an inward sigh of relief as you read. The three phases of Christian maturity discussed in chapters four and five stimulated my mind. My emotions were stirred by a renewed sense of deep joy as I read the extensive description of *agapé* in chapter seven. The tenth chapter is one of the best apologetics for the security of the believer that I have seen. I wish every new Christian would read that chapter within the first months of their new life in Christ.

This first book in the trilogy sets the standard high for the other two. I recommend that you read it, then reflect on its truths. Then read it again. Like any great work of art, the nuances grow richer and deeper with each examination. May this portrait of grace find a prominent place in the gallery of God's Church.

Dr. Steve McVey
President, Grace Walk Ministries

CONTENTS

"Nothing is truly yours until you understand it –
not even yourself."

CHAPTER 1

THE WINE AND
THE WINESKIN

We cannot ignore the fact that there are a growing number of people who used to profess a faith and call themselves Christians but no longer do so. Even higher is the number of people who used to go to church only to end up feeling dejected for going to the Charismatic Disneyland and discovering, to their dismay, that they would never be spiritually tall enough to go on any of the rides. Some leave unable to deal with guilt; others withdraw, not being able to reconcile themselves to the apparent contradictions. The cry that has gone up from the Church is the same plaintiff plea heard in Elijah's day: *"O man of God, there is death in the pot!"* (2 Kings 4:40). However, rather than treat the stew with the healing flour of grace, church leaders of today have all too often insisted that the cure is to simply eat more stew.

Perhaps the greatest presumption of this book will be to offer itself as "flour" for the stew. It is designed as a cure for all who unwittingly gathered the wild gourds of religion (mistaking them for the good news of the gospel of grace), ate them and got sick.

However, because so much of what passes for Christianity today is in fact nothing more than self-improvement based on what Man must do for God instead of what Christ has done for Man, we find it hard to discern between Law (wild gourds) and grace (nourishing herbs).

Only when believers have exhausted their own resources and have no strength left with which to attempt to live the Christian life, and only when they have failed and failed comprehensively at trying to live a holy life by self-effort, are they amenable to the Christ-has-done-it-all message of grace. It is then through pain and disillusionment that they find themselves on the way of grace.

In his landmark book, *The Bridges of God*, Donald McGavran expresses his concern that if the only bridge available is the modern day Church, those seeking to know God are in trouble. Not only is this bridge shaky, worse still, many who escort the God-seekers and act as their guides do not know where they themselves are going. As the Bible reminds us, if the blind lead the blind, both fall into a pit (Matthew 15:14; Luke 6:39). It is precisely the need to provide a bridge and a clearly signed pathway that drives these writings of mine.

I have long believed that the "new wine" (the New Covenant message) needs a new wineskin. (This message, incidentally, can no longer be considered "new" but has been largely forgotten by the modern day Church.) To that end, an increasingly important part of my work is to explore ways of helping believers develop organic and ground-up ways of gathering together – *being* church as opposed to merely *going to* church (i.e., having "church" done for and to them where somebody, normally a professional some-body, tells them what to sing, when to sit, when to stand and what to think, and yet, never teaches them how to think). In the final analysis the wineskin is not a church building or our model of church; it is the container; us, the people, the living stones (1 Peter 2:4-5). It is about how we model church both individually and cor-porately. Whether we meet at 11:00 am on a Sunday, whether we sit in a pew or in a pub, is peripheral to the central point of whether when we meet we are being empowered to grow to our full potential as royal priests able to manifest His (Jesus') self-for-others nature to a world that so desperately needs an authentic expression of Christianity.

Accordingly, the *Until Christ Is Formed* trilogy is designed as resource material for churches and small groups, as well as for individual study. The *Until Christ is Formed* trilogy was initially conceived to provide additional resources for the groups that I have had the pleasure of working with in the USA, Brazil and Finland. In making the material available in book form and to a wider audience I have sought with the help of the New Wine editorial team to ensure that the books are not too parochial whilst at the same time hoping that they will still provoke discussion and stimulate fellowship and deeper levels of connection.

As a church-planter I have a gnawing sense that, for me at least, my church-planting praxis is reminiscent of the self-defeating behaviour of a wasp who, having become trapped in a house, attempts to escape by flying headlong into the closed windows time and time again. Somehow, the wasp imagines that if it keeps on doing the same thing, it will get a different result. Of course, it will not and sadly, neither will we.

On the basis that, in the end, we always need to go back to the beginning, it is sure telling that when God commissioned Adam He did not instruct him to build a church in Eden. Rather, God gave Man dominion over the earth and told Man to cultivate and keep it. What God did was prepare Man for life.

I finally resolved that the church-planters' function is to ensure that the people who they meet and who express a desire to gather together must as a result of their relationship with the church-planter at least:

1. Know Christ *for*, *in* and *as* themselves; it is possible to know more about God and, at the same time, not know God any more.

2. Know how to gather under Christ's headship, i.e., without the need for the church-planters to lead the meetings.

3. Become whole and learn to serve the spiritual community to which they belong.

The *Until Christ Is Formed* trilogy charts the spiritual development of the believer through the Apostle John's three phases of the Christian life as described in 1 John 2:12-14. They are: the Child Phase, the Teenage Phase and the Father Phase. This first book of the trilogy in your hands maps out the all important Child Phase. It is in the formative years where our identity is formed and where our life, to a large extent, is shaped. The behavioural patterns learned in our formative years can be changed, but breaking these patterns and habits can be difficult. It is difficult simply because change is difficult and for lasting change to happen a number of things must converge – people change only when they hurt enough to have to, when they know enough to be able to and when they are loved enough to be empowered to.

I hope that if you hurt through the pages of this book, you will learn enough and come to know the love of God enough to be able to make the necessary changes.

CHAPTER 2

GATHERING IN
THE OUTCASTS

The two things that the Child knows seem simple enough, but they actually are profound. Firstly, the Child knows that his sins have been forgiven and secondly he knows the Father. It has been my experience that few Christians know either of these foundational truths at an experiential level. If you were to ask average believers how many of their sins have been forgiven and on what basis are they forgiven, what do you suppose they would say? And if you were to ask these same people to describe God, how would they define Him?

It has taken me many years to answer those foundational questions. Intellectually, they are easy questions to answer, but at an emotional level they are the most searching questions of all. Perhaps these are questions that you too are turning over in your mind?

There can be no one in history who has had to withstand more character assassination attempts than God the Father and His Son Jesus Christ. Our image of God has been misshaped and disfigured by believers and unbelievers in equal measure. Perhaps you have a view of an austere, remote and capricious God. Perhaps you have felt being outside or even beyond His love, an outcast? If that is you, we are going to have a high old time together. You and me.

For I, my friend, am the outcast of outcasts, one who has been gathered in the Father's embrace and is overwhelmed by the sheer absurdity of His love for us all.

One thing I know beyond doubt is that the Bible is about God's love and that love is most wonderfully displayed among the outcasts. There can be few more precious portraits of grace in the Bible which illustrate God's heart for the outcast as well as Samuel's account of the story of Mephibosheth in 2 Samuel 9. God shows grace to all the Mephibosheths who, crippled in the fall, live in exile and in fear.

King David's heart was not at rest even after he had been securely installed in his kingdom. He had a debt of love which he must discharge. His covenant relationship with his beloved friend, Jonathan, had to be honoured. Love has to love. And so, David summoned his servant, Ziba, and asked him, *"Is there still anyone left of the house of Saul, that I may show him kindness for Jonathan's sake?"* When David learnt from Ziba that there was one left, *"... a son of Jonathan* [who is] *crippled in his feet... "* David wasted no time. He was not deterred by Mephibosheth's condition.

> *"The king [David] said to [Ziba], 'Where is he?' And Ziba said to the king, 'He is in the house of Machir [meaning "sold"] the son of Ammiel, at Lo-debar.'"*
>
> (2 Samuel 9:4)

Mephiboseth had lived in exile there ever since David ascended to the throne. In the flight from the Royal City (alluding to the banishment from the Garden of Eden), Mephiboseth, a young prince, was dropped by his nurse and consequently was crippled in the fall. Now, living an ostracized and secluded life, he had reframed his self-image to such an extent that when David summoned him, the young prince could only see himself through the eyes of his infirmity, i.e., as a pauper.

Then, "Mephibosheth the son of Jonathan, son of Saul, came [with great reluctance I am sure] to David and fell on his face and paid homage. And David said, 'Mephibosheth!'" The ensuing dialogue is poignant. "And [Mephibosheth] answered, 'Behold, I am your servant.'" The crippled and rejected man braced himself as he waited for the gavel of judgement to fall, but instead the voice of covenant love tenderly spoke to him.

"And David said to him, 'Do not fear, for I will show you kindness for the sake of your father Jonathan, and I will restore to you all the land of Saul your father, and you shall eat at my table always.'"

(2 Samuel 9:7)

Many of us relate to God in the same way because we live in the consciousness of our sin and not in the knowledge of His covenant grace and the finished work of the cross. Our felt guilt leads us to be fearful of God and our structures seem to validate that feeling; after all, we reckon, "The fear of God is the beginning of wisdom, isn't it?" Indeed it is, but, (and here is the point) being afraid of God is the beginning of religion and the end of relationship.

The outcast had no means of processing what he had just heard; no more than you and I when we are confronted or, rather, affronted by the mystery of grace.

"And [Mephibosheth] paid homage and said, 'What is your servant, that you should show regard for a dead dog such as I?'"

(2 Samuel 9:8)

Sounds familiar? However, grace waved away the projections of a poor self-image and crippled self-esteem. The Lord prepares a table for us in the presence of our enemies. The blunt truth is that our darkest adversaries are within — our thoughts, our doubts, our fears.

"Then the king called Ziba, Saul's servant, and said to him, 'All that belonged to Saul and to all his house I have given to your master's grandson. And you and your sons and your servants shall till the land for him and shall bring in the produce, that your master's grandson may have bread to eat. But Mephibosheth your master's grandson shall always eat at my table.' Now Ziba had fifteen sons and twenty servants. Then Ziba said to the king, 'According to all that my lord the king commands his servant, so will your servant do.' So Mephibosheth ate at David's table, like one of the king's sons. And Mephibosheth had a young son, whose name was Mica. And all who lived in Ziba's house became Mephibosheth's servants. So Mephibosheth lived in Jerusalem, for he ate always at the king's table. Now he was lame in both his feet."

(2 Samuel 9:9-13)

I can see those little crippled feet swinging under the table with disbelief and delight while their owner incredulously looked on at his son, Mica, whose name tells its own story for "Mica" means "who is like God?" Who indeed!

Moreover, the Lord's resounding response to all the Ethiopian eunuchs who cry, "What can prevent me from being baptized?" is, "Nothing. Come, those who have no money and eat and come, those who are thirsty and drink". This book is written by one such reinstated outcast (i.e. me) and it is about my journey into freedom. My prayer is that your reading this book will enable you to become even more firmly rooted in the unshakeable love of God, resting in the knowledge that you are loved and accepted unconditionally with all your sins, past, present and future having already been forgiven.

CHAPTER 3

ONE CHILD'S JOURNEY INTO FREEDOM

8 September 1984: this was when it first dawned on me that either I did not know how the game was played or that my worst fears had been realized, i.e., God (whose game it was) did not play by His own rules. What happened that day left me believing in God, but not capable of believing God.

I was woken up that morning by my then two-year-old daughter, Louisa, bursting into my room, crying, "Daddy, there's a fire, there's a fire!" The next few hours were a blur. It was 7:40am when Louisa raised the alarm that saved her sister's life. By the time the fire brigade arrived, I had somehow managed to also rescue my eldest, Chantelle, and my youngest daughter, Francesca, from the inferno that was our simple little house.

The emergency services arrived in quick succession. With calm efficiency, the fire brigade got straight to work putting out the fire whilst the ambulance crew spirited Chantelle away to hospital, blue lights flashing and siren screaming as they disappeared at high speed into the distance, shattering the suburban silence. But none of the neighbours seemed to object. Most of them had gathered outside our house and were mucking in as best they could, trying to help or console.

Sometime late morning, though the house fire was dampened, the inferno in my soul still raged unabated. I arrived at the specialist burns unit at Queen Mary's Hospital in Roehampton, London. This would be my second home for the next year or so whilst my eldest daughter underwent skin grafts and various operations. I kept asking myself while driving to the hospital, "Why? Why would God allow that to happen to my little girl? If there had to be a fire, why couldn't it be me in the fire instead?" Unwittingly, I had spoken my first words as an intercessor, but such higher truth was wasted on me then. It would be nearly twenty-years thereafter that I understood, the nature of intercession is to stand in the place of another.

Nothing in life could have prepared me for the sight that greeted me when I was shown into my daughter's hospital room. She was literally mummified in bandages with what seemed like a thousand tubes coming out of her. She was only four years old. She was heavily sedated to ease the pain of the burns. The fire had devoured her. I entered the room as quietly as I could, but Chantelle quickly sensed that I had come in.

"Daddy, is that you?"

"Yes, darling, it's me. Don't worry, Daddy's here now. Everything's going to be okay." I hated the fact that I sounded so unconvincing.

"Daddy, are you all right? I heard you got burnt!"

"Yes, sweetie, I'm okay."

"Daddy, are Louisa and Frankie all right?"

"Yes, baby, they're fine. Now, you get some rest."

"Daddy?"

"Yes, Chantelle?"

"I'm glad you're all right. I love you so much that when I come home, I'm going to buy you some Opal Fruits." Again, a lesson for me here. Love is to think of others before yourself. I could not take it any more. I had to leave the room so I could break down and cry my heart out.

I never doubted that there was a God, but at that moment I could not accept that He was good and, for sure, I thought He was not being fair. He had some explaining to do. That day in the hospital I concluded that God did not love me and that He did not care for the things I most valued or, worse, He could not even take care of them. I surmized that either He was able to help me, but did not want to, or He wanted to help me, but was not able to. The first thought made me angry and the second thought made me feel anxious but neither thought made me feel safe. Little did I know then that I would give my life to helping people whose life and church experiences had led them to arrive at a similar premise about God.

A premise is a condition or statement presumed to be true from which a conclusion is drawn. So, if you will, a premise is a presupposition. Now, if your premise is wrong, any conclusion drawn from that premise will also be wrong. My premise about God was fatally flawed at that point of time.

After the fire I decided that if I could not trust God to look after my baby, I could not trust God. Full stop. The more I thought about it, the more I had to accept that His record of protecting me and what was mine was not exactly anything to be proud of and that perhaps my trust in Him was misplaced in any case (more on this later). After some soul searching, I decided that whilst I did believe in God, I could not believe that if He loved me, He would let such dreadful things keep happening to me. A new thought dawned on me: maybe I was the problem; maybe I was not worth loving or protecting; maybe I was unlovable. The more I thought about it, the more it became apparent that this must be the right answer.

I have observed that it is not so much what happens to me that is harmful, but rather it is my view of what has happened that causes me the most distress.

Life's events, it seems, prompt impulses deep inside of us that cause us to either open up or close down. My childhood was full of unwelcome surprises. In the next book in this series,

The Apprentice, I will share with you how something which happened to me when I was forty-five days old took me more than forty-five years to recover from. In our formative years, events and circumstances that happen to us cause us to either trust or mistrust. I knew better than to trust, especially those who were supposed to take care of me.

In my teenage years, though I craved intimacy more than anything, nothing terrified me more than the thought of being intimate. All I could feel was despair. That was how my journey into freedom began. It would take many years but eventually, that disdain which so gripped me would become learning. An inner-knowing from recognising that all progress in the Christian life is predicated on disillusionment would come.

The Stage	The Impulse	The Consequence
Child	Trust vs. Mistrust	= Hope or withdrawal
Teenager	Intimacy vs. Isolation	= Other-love or Self-love
Fatherhood	Dignity vs. Despair	= Learning or Disdain

The journey into freedom in Christ begins and can only begin when we place our confidence in God. As I had some trust issues with God, it meant that I had to retrace each increasingly self-protective step that I had made away from Him. Instead of a tactical withdrawal from God, I needed to move towards Him in hope. Instead of the pseudo-safety of isolation, I needed to embrace what seemed like the near death experience of intimacy.

It was a lot to ask; perhaps too much. For that to happen I would need to resolve the most fundamental of questions: Can I trust God?

A few years ago the Lord spoke to me saying, "Paul, you have spent the last five years teaching people about who they are in Christ but what I need you to do is to tell them about who I am." Initially I was a little taken aback, but the more I thought about it, the more I realized that this is the great need in the Church today.

We simply do not know who God is and worse still, in the absence of any true knowing, we have substituted *the God who is* for a god who is made in our own image and likeness. We have allowed the evangelical Aarons to fashion God into a molten calf and this god we have come to worship is not the God of the Bible but a warped caricature, a perversion of God and, dare I say it, even an anti-Christ in many circles. I understand that that is emotive language and I hesitated before saying it; yet, it is important for me to speak plainly. The "God" of much of modern "Christianity" is depicted as being angry or, at best, withholding His anger. He is a God obsessed with sin, apparently.

In spite of all we know about the cross, God is presented as a god we need to fear and since this god is holy and unapproachable, we must live lives which please Him. Such is the malaise in modern evangelical Christianity that I am bold enough to say that what we have been raised on is Christianity without Christ. My desire is to restore the Church to her true pure state, i.e., Christ without Christianity. If we were to remove the "-ianity" (the "insanity") from "Christianity", what we are left with is Christ and Christ is but one thing and one thing only – Love!

It may have been twenty-years to the day after the fire that I walked the grounds of a retreat centre, having been set by the retreat facilitator an assignment I was reluctantly complying with. We, a group of church leaders, were given an exercise about "purpose" and, a somewhat reluctant participant, I made my way into the grounds. There the Lord spoke to me saying, "Your purpose is to fulfil the G.R.A.C.E. Co-Mission." I smiled because, as a former Pentecostal, I knew all about the so-called Great Commission. The Lord knew He had my attention and continued, "From now on, 'grace' is an acronym for you; it means 'God's Ridiculous *Agapé* Captivating Everyone'." I was enchanted.

Now, if you are having some difficulty reconciling my murderous thoughts in the hospital with my vocational reflections in a Retreat Centre somewhere in leafy Buckinghamshire, don't worry, it will all become clear. You see, unlike the man from the Commercial Union Insurance company who having only seven days prior to the fire insured our property and its contents made good on their promise that they would never make a drama out of a crisis, God uses our crises as an opportunity to unfold the drama of redemption – the story of His unfailing love for us. It is my prayer that through the drama and various crises of my life that you too will be captivated by God's Ridiculous Love for you.

In Cognitive Therapy, counsellors seek to alleviate their clients' emotional distress by helping them to identify, examine and modify the distorted and maladaptive thinking underlying their distress. Essentially, the therapist helps their clients to challenge their own premise and reframe their fundamental underlying assumptions about certain situations that are causing them anxiety and discomfort.

Twenty-five years on from that dreadful flaming September morning, I still have the picture of Chantelle looking up at me through the bandages. Today, I am beginning to understand that part of the reason for my total breakdown was that I was looking back at her through the veil ... "but when one turns to the Lord, the veil is removed" (2 Corinthians 3:16).

The book that you have in your hands is really a book designed to challenge you to rethink your premise about God by challenging your fundamental underlying assumptions about Him and the basis of the Christian message.

CHAPTER 4

ADOPTION
ASSURANCE

Ralph Waldo Emmerson is reported to have greeted friends whom he had not seen for some time with the question, "What has become clear to you since the last time we met?" Were I asked that question by any of my old friends from my formative Christian years, I would answer unequivocally that the one thing which has become clear to me is the relationship between God and Man. It is not at all what I had first come to know, but I daresay that I may never fathom the true depths and possibilities of it this side of heaven.

To begin with, I had previously assumed that Christianity was a religion. A religion based on rules. I had supposed that it was trans-actional i.e., if I put in 'x' I could expect to take 'y' out. But to my delight, I discovered that it is not a religion at all, but a relationship based on unconditional love.

In a moment, I will begin to explain the somewhat unorthodox way in which I came to be persuaded of this truth. The journey that takes us from calculation to contemplation requires that we go through our individual valley of Baca (Psalm 84) and in that place of worry and dismay discover how so often that is through overwhelming sorrow and loss that we find Him. The Spirit leads us out of our wilderness to be confronted by obstacles that our egos and our ingenuity simply cannot overcome in and of their own strength. However, when such an unwelcome intruder comes in like a flood and we wave our white flag of surrender, the Holy Spirit raises His standard and we are moved from mere cognition to recognition. Job-like, Jacob-like we are all alike in this regard I suspect. We discover treasure hidden in the darkness. I know that I am unconditionally loved and accepted and have been forgiven of all my sins, past, present and future. I am safe and sound and am one spirit with Him, but more recently I have come to see that there is more to the Christian life. Much, much more. Christianity is as much about destiny as it is about destination. We are heirs of God, but as the Apostle Paul puts it in his letter to the Galatians,

> *"I mean that the heir, as long as he is a child, is no different from a slave, though he is the owner of everything, but he is under guardians and managers until the date set by his father."*
>
> (Galatians 4:1-2)

Many of us who have embraced the grace message are only too aware that the one thing worse than seeing the message of freedom go unused is to see it misused. We are charting a straight course between the ship-wrecking icebergs of anything-goes-license and nothing-goes-legalism; we are heading for the place of response-ability (being able to respond, it is the grace of God that helps us to say no to unrighteousness Titus 2:11) where we exchange a child-ish faith for a childlike one.

How the child-heir comes to maturity and thus accesses his inheritance and exercises his authority is the essence of the *Until Christ Is Formed* trilogy series of which this book is a part. The Child's journey will be charted through the three phases of the Christian life as set out by the Apostle John in 1 John 2:12-14. These stages he enumerates as being the Child, Teenage and Father phases.

Looking back these forty years, I confess I had never realized at the time that the single most important lesson I would ever learn about the nature of God I would learn across the breakfast table as a nine-year old boy. Although it took me more than two decades to fully understand its significance, that lesson became the cornerstone of my faith in Christ.

Let me tell you what happened.

Once upon a time there was a boy. Me. I was a happy and popular child. Although I showed little interest in academic subjects, I excelled at sports. I lived in what was then a pleasant but sleepy little town in Surrey called Addlestone, south-west of London and just south of Heathrow Airport. Far more interesting places lay beyond Addlestone's boundaries like Chertsey, Weybridge, Byfleet and Guilford. I would often watch the Red Rover buses and the quaint little single-deckers (with their luxurious seats) pass the house displaying their destinations on the front and I wondered what it would be like to visit these "far off" places.

However, Addlestone was not without its distractions. There was plenty to occupy an outward-bound nine-year-old. Together with my friends, Gerard and Peter, we would play all day in the parks, the ponds, the woods and, of course, the railway bridge where we would dare each other to run across the bridge when the train passed under it and we would disappear in the smoke billowing out of the chimney of the departing train. Then, on the rare occasion when I was not out with my friends playing football, there were my elder brothers, Patrick and Desmond, to play with. There was also my sister, Maureen, during the rare moments that she would prise herself away from her Beatles collection. Yet, the best and most diverting of all was my being able to go to work with my father every other Saturday. That was until he took ill and had to take early retirement. Yes, life was good with not a cloud in the sky or, at least, it was good until one particular night when I would learn my most profound lesson about the nature of God.

It was 1969 and yet I remember it as though it was yesterday. I had gone to bed and as was my usual ritual, I watched the car head-lights course across my room. The headlights would chase up the wall and across the ceiling, flooding the room with light, and then, run down the other wall before disappearing. The roar of the cars would fade as the drivers of the cars made their way to somewhere more exotic than Addlestone. I would often imagine the stories of those driving the cars. Sometimes I would weave very elaborate tales about who they were and what they were up to. Spies were my big thing at the time and thus, most of my fictitious characters were Secret Agents off on some daring mission.

It was an audacious mission of sorts which caused a car to come to an abrupt halt outside of our house about an hour after I had gone to bed. I had watched, as usual, the car's headlight crawl up the far wall, but to my surprise, rather than tracing its familiar jour-ney it stayed there for a moment and then vanished. How bizarre! So intrigued was I that I climbed out of bed and peered out of my window to see what was going on. Furtively, I pulled back the corner of my curtain in time to see two people getting out of the car and heading towards our front gate. Their car doors had been shut with a resolute thud! The man motioned the woman towards our gate and she, slightly gingerly, opened it. She seemed to brace herself (psyching herself up the way a trainee door-to-door sales-man making his first house call might) before striding up the path. The man stayed back and remained at the gate. She rung the bell and rapped the knocker simultaneously. Big mistake – my mother did not like disturbances. It was my mother who opened the door. I was surprised when the doorstep conversation ensued for sev-eral moments. The longer the conversation went on, the louder and more agitated the muffled sounds became.

Whatever was going on downstairs it was not to be missed! I decided to creep down the landing and peer down the stairs to get a better vantage point. When I arrived there, to my surprise, Desmond was already there.

"Shhh ... go back to bed," he said before I had had a chance to say anything or make any noise.

"Who is it?" I whispered, choosing to ignore him.

"I don't know. It's a mad woman and she's demanding to see me," Desmond replied.

I could just make her out. I had never seen her before. She stood in front of my mother who framed the door, forbidding entry. My mother had been joined by my father at the door. I had not noticed until then how frail he looked. He was a shadow of his former self. He had been ill for some time now and we saw less and less of him as he spent more and more time confined to bed in the downstairs parlour. He was no longer able to climb the stairs. Supported by his walking-frame, my father had gone to lend his support to my mother. This must be serious!

"I know my rights," the woman demanded. "He's my ..."

"You have no rights!" my mother boomed, drowning out the woman's voice. "But I'll give you this – you've a brass neck coming here!"

With that, my mother slammed the door in the woman's face, turned on her heels and, without even shooting a glance at us, said, "And you two, go back to bed!" How did adults know things like that? I had always suspected that my mother had eyes in the back of her head. Desmond and I scurried off to bed.

The man and the woman did not leave immediately. I watched them from a tiny corner in my curtain which I had pulled back. They were locked in earnest debate on the front garden path. The man seemed to be encouraging her to leave. After some moments she did, but not before kicking over a number of my mother's plant pots. With that, they left.

The house fell quiet. I could only imagine what Desmond must have been thinking as he lay in his bed, rehearsing the strange events which had just played out.

"He's my ..."

"'He's my what?" I wondered. You could be sure that I would question my mother about this in the morning.

There was an uncharacteristic sense of unease at the breakfast table. Desmond and I sat alone. Our mother occupied herself with other chores. She was clearly avoiding us. Desmond did not seem to be too keen to engage her either. I, on the other hand, was possessed of a refreshing gaucheness.

"Mother, who's that lady who came to the house last night?"

"That's no lady," she snapped.

"Why did she kick the flower pots over?"

"It doesn't concern you, Paul. It's adult stuff. Besides, you're late for school."

I kicked Desmond under the table. "Go on! Ask her, you fool!" my face demanded.

Desmond cleared his throat. "Ma ...?" Desmond always called her "Ma" when he was trying to inveigle his way into her favours. "What did the lady mean when she said, 'He's my ...'?"

My mother knew it was useless. Besides, she had no right to withhold the information she had kept to herself all these years. She undid her apron and sat down beside us.

"Boys," she said, "I've something to tell you." She hesitated and then, "Although you're both my sons, you're not my sons."

She had begun esoterically, continuing in her tautological explanation and then, she corrected herself. "Well, actually, Desmond is."

She seemed very muddled, but I guessed that there was no way to say this kind of stuff easily. "What I mean is," she said, composing herself, "Desmond, you're not my natural son. You're my adopted son. That means that you're as good as my own child; if not, even more so because legally, you're mine. As to my legal responsibilities, ironically, you have more rights than Jill and Jean, my real children."

My head was spinning. "What on earth was unravelling in front of my eyes?!" It was clear that we had yet to get to the bottom line (at least, from my perspective).

My mother continued, "The woman who came last night was your natural mother. She came to take you away, but I sent her packing because you're not her child any more." It was as if a great weight had been lifted from her shoulders.

Desmond was four years older than I am. He sat there dumfounded. "You're not my mother!" he exclaimed.

"No, Desmond, I am your mother. That's the point."

The revelation was too much for Desmond to process. He got up and began to leave the kitchen.

My mother exclaimed after him, "It's all right, Desmond, don't worry, you're safe and sound with us. You're not going anywhere, nobody can ever take you away!"

The kitchen door slammed shut and moments later we heard his footsteps stamping upstairs above our heads. I looked at my mother demandingly. At that point, her attacking me seemed the best form of defence and I thought that I would surely be in for it for having opened Pandora's box. Yet, my mother was not angry with me. No, the disclosure seemed to have liberated her somehow. She looked relieved. Instead, she put her hand on mine and said, "Paul, I'm only grateful that it wasn't your mother who came last night, because if it had been, I would have to give you back. You see, son, Desmond is adopted, you're only fostered. Your father and I have lived in fear of losing you all these years. You've been with us since you were three months old. Mrs Damen, your social worker, says that we've nothing to worry about. Your parents will never come for you, not after abandoning you like that."

My foster mother spoke as if I was aware that I had been abandoned at birth. Like in the tale of Chicken Licken, the sky had fallen in.

The words "son" and "your father" seemed to me to be an inappropriate choice of words at that time. As for Mrs Damen, I thought that she was my aunty. But, come to think of it, she used to frequently see me in the parlour and also in private, ask a whole load of questions and always had a large blue notebook.

Within a year my life changed radically. Events would so conspire against me that I would get to know places way beyond the destinations written on the front of the buses which trundled past that old house on Brighton Road, Addlestone. My foster mother's revelations had shattered the tranquillity. Not too many months after that, my foster father lost his battle with cancer, passing peacefully in his sleep.

My foster mother passed away some time later, it may well have been on Maunday Thursday, i.e., the day before Good Friday in the Catholic calendar. At her bedside, my foster mother summoned Desmond and me to talk with us. We had not the slightest inkling what she was going to say and, even less so, that her time to go Home had come.

Desmond spoke with my foster mother first. Ever since that great revelation she had been very tender to Desmond and he had been a little withdrawn. He loved her very much and was a happy boy. He had no desire to know the strange woman who had banged on our door that night a year ago. My foster mother kept Desmond at her side for some time. I could just about hear their conversation. She seemed to be making arrangements with him as she kept talking about provision.

Then she said, "It's all arranged. The majority of what I have is yours." This was getting interesting. Not so very long ago, before that cataclysmic night, I had been given Desmond's pocket-money because my foster mother had said that he was lazy. So, if she was giving out presents, I thought to myself, I was going to do okay here. Desmond got up and came over to me. He was tearful.

"What?" I whispered, "What's going on?" Desmond did not say a word but just motioned me to her bedside.

I ventured close to my foster mother, a little apprehensively, and said, "Mum?"

"Sit down, Paul. I must tell you something. I don't have long."
I duly sat down, gripped with a sense of foreboding. I could not
help thinking how weak she looked, how tired she seemed.

Mrs Growney, my friend Gerard's real mother, hovered in the
background. "Go on, Iris," she encouraged my foster mother.

"Paul, I'm dying. It won't be long now. When I die, you'll be
going to an orphanage. A good one, mind, with very kind people to
take care of you. You're going to like it there."

I was not listening. My foster mother was dying and I was as
good as dead. When I sat down next to her bed earlier on, I was
Paul Walsh, a ten-year-old who worried if anybody were to call
at my house lest it be my biological mother and suddenly I was
Oliver Twist. The crash of the collision between these two new
realities was deafening and immobilising.

Sadly, it was an air bubble in a blood transfusion which ushered
in my foster mother's homecoming. I only saw her a few times
after the bedside summit and then she was gone. With her parting,
I felt that I would have to fend for myself in an unfriendly world.
Maureen, my big sister, came to close the house up. Eventually, after waiting for a while following the house closing,
my new social worker arrived to take Desmond and me to our
short-stay foster home. In a few months, Desmond was spirited away to his new life and I was in a car en route to Enfield,
Middlesex, which would be my home for the next seven years.
That first night in Enfield, I lay in my bed, hugging my Bible.
I had never read it before then, but it was bequeathed to me
by my foster mother together with £50.00 of National Savings
Certificates. I was not sure why she had given it to me, but
that night I was so glad she had. I hugged it for all I was worth
and through my tears I said, "If You're real, God, and You care
about little boys, I really need Your help as I don't think I can
make it here."

My induction into the orphanage had brought with it truly
shocking revelations. They came thick and fast in those days.

The day for me to be sent off to the orphanage arrived one afternoon in July 1970. Kate, my short-term foster mother, had driven me there from my temporary home in Kenton. The day before she had taken me to Sopers, a department store in Harrow-on-the-Hill, and bought me a smart new outfit. Chocolate brown flared trousers, a beige shirt and a rainbow-coloured tank top. Very fetching, I seem to recall; give me a break here, it was the 70's – what else could it be?!

As we made our way to the orphanage I peered glumly out of the car window, wondering whether I would ever see Desmond again. We arrived sooner than I had hoped. It was early afternoon. I was numb. The house was not what I had imagined it to be. It was a large modern detached townhouse, No. 221, Holtwhites Hill, called *Carmel*.

A smart knock on the door brought an African lady by the name of Agnes to the front door. She smiled warmly, "You must be Paul. Welcome. Come in."

Kate ushered me across the daunting threshold. The door closed firmly behind her. The house was empty. Agnes explained that the children were at the park. "Shame you didn't arrive earlier. You could've gone with them."

She motioned for us to enter the parlour. Once we were seated she offered tea and biscuits. The handover took about an hour. I was not sure whose benefit it was for, mine or Kate's. Anyway, before too long, Kate was gone as well. From the window of the house I watched as she drove away. I would stand at that same window many times in the following years, watching people go and waiting for people to come.

By teatime the other children returned from their adventures in the park. What an unruly shower! I had never seen such a motley crew. The entire household gathered in the sitting-room to meet their new "inmate."

"What's your name?"

"Who'd you support?"

"Why'd ya parents dump ya?"

"How old are ya?"

"D'you reckon you're 'ard?"

"Got any good stuff?"

I was in Hell. I was sure of it. I surveyed my inquisitors. They were a rainbow coalition of demandingness. Black, white, Mediterranean et al. The boys squealed with amusement as I attempted to answer their questions with a polite well-manicured Surrey accent which needed to be abandoned if I was planning to survive into my teenage years.

"Paul."

"Manchester United."

"I'm not sure but my other parents died."

"I'm 10 years old. I'll be 11 in February."

"What does 'ard' mean?"

"Yes, I've got World Cup stickers, some Paddington Books, a Bobby Brewster collection and I once had a conker that was a 103." (It seemed worthwhile trying to claim some bragging rights, but that was about the extent of the asset inventory and since I did not feel it prudent to disclose the £50.00 at this stage, I left it at that.)

The boys were in hysterics.

"Why'dew speak posh?" the tallest and most menacing of the boys demanded. "Are you a poof?"

Before I could address both questions a rather more pressing matter arose. It was the menacing boy again, "You ain't allowed to support Man United. Around 'ere, it's either Spurs or Arsenal or you get ya 'ead kicked in."

I decided to ignore the first question and given that I did not know what a "poof" was, I would avoid that question as well although, intuitively, I suspected that an indignant "No, I'm not!" would be a good answer to question number two. It was the question of allegiance to a football team which I immediately understood at that moment. It would grieve me to give up my beloved Manchester United. I had been a Georgie Best fan for as long as I could remember. Furthermore, Manchester United had just won the European Cup and my foster mother had let me stay up to watch the game. I had sat there, screaming at the television in my Bobby Charlton pyjamas. Giving up Manchester United was a lot to ask. Moreover, I suspected that it was also a trick question and that the wrong choice between Spurs and Arsenal would land me in trouble. As it turned out, Kate, a mad Spurs supporter, had taken me to see the Spurs during my brief stay with her. I loved that game and Spurs trounced Nottingham Forest 4-1. I did not care much for Arsenal and so I took a chance and said, "Spurs." A great roar broke out. I was in! Acceptance. How sweet the feeling was!

We learn to cope, don't we? Life is about adapting and surviving. I was a survivor, a chameleon, and changing my colour to suit my environment would soon become a way of life.

I had pondered most of the afternoon whether to speak to one of the nuns in charge of the orphanage about my concerns. I did not think that I had too much to lose and thus I asked for a meeting. I was shepherded into the parlour.

"Yes, Paul, what is it? How are you getting on?"

"Well," I began with all the gravitas a ten-year-old can muster, "I'm not sure if I can stay here."

"Oh, really?" replied Sister Angela with feigned concern. "Why is that?"

"Well, I don't think I really fit in."

There was a pause. Clearly, that statement required further elucidation.

"Everybody here is coloured," I said. The slight overstatement was for effect.

"Oh, I see," said Sister Angela, trying to suppress a grin. "Umm … I've some news for you, young man, which may help you to settle in here – so are you! Your father's from the Caribbean and your mother's from Ireland and so you fit right in!"

I was dumbfounded. Right there in that little parlour, the sky fell in a second time. Three questions, the existential ones, exploded in my mind ...

"Who am I?"

"Where did I come from?"

"What the hell am I doing here?"

I would have to wait until I was thirty-five to discover the answer to those questions. In the meantime I would proceed through life as an acceptance addict, desperate to be loved and yet afraid of intimacy for fear that those whom I loved had an ugly habit of leaving me. I would go out of my way to please people for fear that displeasing them would result in rejection. In addition, I was being raised in a Catholic Convent while being educated in a Jesuit College and thus, I had my fair share of Catholic guilt to contend with too. On top of all that I had to try and figure out this colour issue. I was, in short, mixed race and mixed up. In any event I had, at least, resolved the puzzling question of why my hair grew upwards while everyone else's in my "family" grew downwards. Whilst theirs seemed to fall into place naturally, mine required a liberal application of Brylcreem hair-cream to keep it in place. This would prove to be a prophetic indicator.

Life in the orphanage was not without its advantages once one had worked out the rhythm of the place. It had its rules, as I would imagine a young offenders institute might have. In such places, you fight your way to the top. It was kind of like the law of the jungle. I was good at sports; I was a natural leader; I had oodles of charm; and the mums of potential suitors were always well disposed to me. But the other boys were street-hardened. I was academically brighter, but had none of their sheer mental strength. They were numb to physical pain. They had been institutionalized all their lives. They had guile and savvy, the kind which one might well associate with the Artful Dodger. I had none of that but had a winsome way with people.

Seven years in an orphanage had a way of shaping the world for
an orphan. By the time I was seventeen, I left the home and went
reluctantly into the world, not to make my fortune but simply to
survive. Within two years I was married and in another seven, I
was divorced.

I sat alone in our house in the stockbroker belt of Surrey (I had
promised myself that I would make it back there someday) and
wept. I was alone again, but this time with four children under the
age of eight to raise. However, unbeknownst to me at that time, all
spiritual progress begins with disillusionment. I was ready. The
ground had been prepared.

In September 2004, at a time when Hayley and I were developing
The Grace Project in a particular direction, the Lord led us to find
a new home for the project. The place we identified seemed to fit
the specifications we had received from the Lord: "You are to find
a white building with plenty of glass."

One Sunday, as Hayley and I were making our way to our
church meeting, we happened upon a building which caught
our attention. When we arrived at the meeting place, something strange happened. One of the sisters had brought with
her a bag full of flags and deposited them at the front of the
meeting place. During the meeting people came and took the
flags, each one seemingly able to assign a prophetic value to
the flag they had chosen. All the flags, with the exception of a
fuschia pink one, were picked up. As the unwanted flag lay on
the floor the Lord spoke to me about it: "Education and Arts."
That was it.

The following morning, having booked an appointment to view
the building we "chanced" upon the previous day, I was praying
and the Lord spoke to me again: "Custard Pie Factory." I do not
know about you, but I find that He can be a little obtuse when He

wants to be. I was puzzled but concluded that He wanted me to go to Birmingham to view a space which a group called Artisan used and was called the Custard Pie Factory. I would make the call later. Thinking no more of it, I made my way to the viewing appointment.

I was greeted by a most genial general manager who would show me the property. To my stunned amazement, when he opened the main doors, the sight I saw almost knocked me over. The floor of the property was the same shade of fuschia pink as the unwanted flag from the meeting the day before. I gulped, trying to suppress my enthusiasm. I mean, how do you explain that to a commercial manager? Anyway, we viewed the appointed studio.

I asked the manager, "Tell me, what was this place before you converted it?"

"Ummm," he said matter-of-factly, "it was a custard pie factory."

"Oh. We'll take it. Where do we sign?" I answered.

A few days later, having had the chance to think about it, my faith was waning as it was wont to do whenever new financial obligations were assumed. God spoke gently to me again, "Son, which part of 'pink floors' and 'custard pie factory' didn't you understand? Go back to the building again today and I'll show you something." I called the general manager again and made some excuse to revisit.

With my being left alone in the studio, the Lord spoke to me again, "Where are you?"

I thought better than giving the obvious answer. Then, He called to my remembrance the prophecy which my friend, Carrie, had given me all those years ago:

*"Thus says the Lord: 'In a time of favour I have answered you; in a day of salvation I have helped you; **all these years, throughout all the tears, I have kept you and given you** as a covenant to the people, to establish the land, to apportion the desolate heritages.'"*

(Isaiah 49:8; bold words indicate the

prophetic personalization of the scripture)

"Son, you're standing less than four hundred yards from the spot where you were abandoned by your real mother."

And so, I was. I had no idea that this was where the Park Royal Hospital had stood before it was pulled down.

"Son, this is part of your desolate heritage. It's your time. This is the time of favour. It's time for you to say to the prisoners, 'Come out'; to those who are in darkness, 'Show yourselves.'"

CHAPTER 5

LOVED AND ACCEPTED

"Eliza Doolittle married Freddy Eynsford-Hill because she knew that she would always be a cockney flower girl to Professor Henry Higgins. She knew that he could never accept the change in her but would always see her as she used to be. As she told Freddy, 'The difference between a lady and a flower girl is not how she behaves but how she is treated. I shall always be a flower girl to Professor Higgins because he always treats me as a flower girl and always will; but I know I can be a lady to you because you always treat me as a lady and always will."

Pygmalion, George Bernard Shaw

Sooner or later, every believer must confront two most foundational of questions:

"Does God accept me?"

"And if so, on what basis does He do so?"

Therefore, let me ask you, when you think of your relationship with God, do you think that He sees you as Henry Higgins saw Eliza Doolittle or as Freddy Eynsford-Hill saw her? Well, let me be bold to suggest to you, Miss Eliza Need-do-nothing-at-all, that when God sees us, He sees us as His bride.

You are to God what Rachel was to Jacob; never his Leah but always his beloved Rachel. Yet, acceptance is such a deeply rooted problem in the mind of Man that even someone like Rachel, who was adored by her husband Jacob, was convinced that her husband would love her more if only she was able to give him a child. The story of Rachel and Leah is, in many respects, one of the more melancholic stories in the Old Testament. Leah, Jacob's wife, by virtue of her father's duplicity, sought to win the heart of her husband by giving him children (typical of good works). Indeed, at the birth of her third son she pronounced, *"'Now this time my husband will be attached to me, because I have borne him three sons,' and his name was called Levi"* (Genesis 29:34). It is surely the heavy hand of irony which sees Levi become the priestly tribe of the law of self-effort. The principle that God will surely love us more if only we could produce some good works is embedded in the religious mind. Even Rachel, who knew beyond doubt that she was loved unconditionally, was still snared in the light of her sister's productivity. Envy had taken root inside of her (Genesis 30:1). Rachel was barren but, driven by the insatiable sense of "I know you love me but ..." she demanded of her husband to "give me children, or I shall die!" (Genesis 30:1).

As with her mother-in-law before her, she reached out with the arm of the flesh to resolve her predicament and presented her maid, Bilhah (whose name means 'foolish', ironically) to her husband who duly provided her with a surrogate child. Yet, whilst Rachel drew consolation from her child, she completely missed the mystery of grace, as so many of us do. In this case, she missed the fact that Jacob would not love Leah any more because of her good works and not love Rachel any less in spite of her lack of works. Grace does not function like that.

Failure to accept that we are loved and accepted unconditionally effectively torpedoes our relationship with God. If we cannot be certain that we are accepted, how do we know what is expected and what will and will not be inspected? The moment we set foot down that road, our relationship with God is infected.

Until this gnawing issue is resolved, the prospect of entering into the Hebrews 4 rest will elude a believer. Our understanding of acceptance must be the same as God's. The Bible is clear – we are *accepted* by the Father *in Christ* (Ephesians 1:6 NASB). Now having said that I know that there is a danger that those of us who have been reared on fear will hear even this liberating truth the wrong way. Let me explain it to you in an anti-parable.

Many years ago I remember going to an exclusive West End night club with a friend of mine who was at that time a high profile Premiership Football player; (now that he has retired he is an even higher profile broadcaster). We arrived at the club and were confronted by a forbidding thou-shalt-not-pass looking doorman. Upon seeing my friend his countenance changed dramatically. Immediately he softened to a jelly like substance. "Evening Garth." He fawned and then wanting to clarify if we were together or whether I was some interloper attempting to slipstream my way into the exclusive nightclub gestured inquiringly towards me. In this unspoken code that obviously both Garth and this Goliath were familiar with Garth nodded approvingly in my direction. In an instant without a word of exchange between the two men the red sea of celebrity access all areas opened up before me. I was in. I was accepted in the be-loved Browns nightclub.

A couple of months later I was again in Covent Garden, though this time I was with Hayley. We had just had a very satisfactory dinner somewhere and I thought I would en-cash a dividend from my new found socialite status and impress her by getting into my new club. I figured that so long as the same guy was on the door, we'd be fine. We duly presented ourselves at the door of the nightclub and with a confident knock at the door I waited for my man to appear.

A few moments passed and no door opened so I knocked again. "Must be the music," I unconvincingly suggested to Hayley. When the door did finally open, it did so reluctantly. And when it did its entire frame was filled by my 'friend' the Goliathian chap from the month before. However, this time there was a noticeable absence of any bonhomie. Gone was the warmth that had greeted me when I was with Garth. Now just an icy blast. I'd come this far, so I decided to press-in. "Hi, how are you?" The doorman, obviously afflicted by some temporary form of amnesia, starred at me blankly. "Members only" he said, and closed the door... As the door slammed shut to my extended night out so my fame-by-association-credibility drowned along with my Pharaoh's army of my social elevation.

"But I am Garth's friend," I protested to the firmly shut door. "I was here with him last month."

The door swung open again.

I straightened up. It was my friend again.. With a chilling economy he clarified the position for me: "Get lost."

The door closed again. I realized that if I ever wanted to go back there then I'd better be sure to go with Garth or one of my other celebrity chums because on my own I would not be accepted.

Now that's the point. It is not like that with God. We are not accepted only when we turn-up with Jesus. He loves us because of who we are not because of who we're with. He loves us in our own right. God the Father is not like some step-grandfather who puts up with us because his son took on someone else's kids. We're not tolerated step-children; we are co-equal, co-heirs with Christ.

Acceptance in Christ is not like that; it is based on one thing – perfection (Matthew 5:48). Whose? Not ours but His! It is not so much that we are in Christ but rather, *Christ is in us*. He has made us perfect forever (Hebrews 10:14). He is our life (Colossians 3:4) and our righteousness (2 Corinthians 5:21). Jesus did not just live His life *for* you. He lived it *as* you. He died for you then, so that He could live in you and as you now. Consequently, when the Father sees you and me, He sees Him (*cf.* John 14:20).

Even those of us who purport to rest in the love of God have a tendency to secretly believe that God would accept us *more* if we were more like X, Y or Z. Every Christian owns at least one pair of "Levi's". This unease is reinforced by our discipleship programmes which consist of somebody telling us what we can, cannot, should and should not do, rather than just telling us who we are! Sadly, this *less-than-Jesus* discipleship is the inevitable by-product of less-than-Jesus evangelism – the kind where salvation amounts to a person getting their past sins forgiven.

Salvation is not getting your sins forgiven, it is receiving His life (John 10:10). It is about what happens in you when you realize and appropriate the love of God. It is the pilgrimage from *induction* to *reproduction*.

We Christians are not people who change our lives with God's help. We are a supernatural people who have exchanged our lives – ours for His – by God's grace without any help from us. We, therefore, are saved not by His death but by His resurrected life (Romans 5:10). We cannot experientially have one without the other, but it is imperative that we do not confuse one with the other. His death is the preamble to our receiving His *zoë* life, i.e., life as God has it in and of Himself.

How far removed this is from our idea of the Christian life which we feel pressured to give witness to and wonder why our clumsy guilt-stained efforts yield such meagre results. In reality, there seem to be only two groups of people on earth – those who live a life they do not have and those who have a life they do not live.

The latter has nothing to attract the former. "Why," asks the world, "should we come to your church? It looks like it's killing you!" If only it was! But the truth is that in having substituted religion for relationship and Christianity for Christ, there is nothing abundant about religion apart from the interminable boredom and the ever-present anxiety.

Thus, mine is a plaintive plea to see the reintroduction of a third group – one which comprises people who consider themselves dead (Romans 6:11), knowing that for them, *"to live is Christ"* (Philippians 1:21) and that Christ is their life (Colossians 3:4).

After all, the Great Commission does not say "do witnessing", it says, "*be* witnesses."

If twenty years in sales and marketing taught me anything, it taught me this – you cannot sell anything to anyone, but what you can do is create in someone a desire to buy. It is only when we let Christ live His *zoë* life through us that we become unconscious participants in a truly effective "witness programme", unearthing a vast number of people wanting to know how they too can "Get A Life". Thus, this book is offered to assist people in finding the divine life which lives within them but, for most, remains dormant.

CHAPTER 6

GROWING IN GRACE

At the heart of our discussions in this series of books is my belief that Christians do not seem to grow to their full potential because their development has been arrested by failing to ever truly understand the nature of the Christian identity. In this trilogy, I hope to demonstrate that as believers we must pass through these phases – Childhood, Adolescence and Fatherhood. At each stage we are to appropriate the tremendous life lessons before proceeding to take the next sequential step. This linear progression will have the glorious effect of taking us from having confidence in God to becoming *confidants* of God, from being safe as sons to being *safe sons*. However, these phases must not be rushed as though Fatherhood is the end goal. That has been one of Mankind's greatest mistakes. No, each phase is to be cherished and savoured with the destination being the journey.

This trilogy is about that journey and, as we shall see, it is a journey into freedom. May you embrace it, find peace and experience an ever deepening understanding of what is.

The Three Phases of Grace
I have often thought that the Apostle John's First Epistle not only contains one of the most misapplied verses in the entirety of

Scripture, but also some of its most overlooked verses. I am referring, of course, to Chapter 1 Verse 9:

> *"If we confess our sins, He is faithful and just to forgive us
> our sins and to cleanse us from all unrighteousness."*

More of that later, but suffice for now to say that there are some compelling reasons why we simply cannot link confession together with
forgiveness in the life of a believer. The Christian's obsession with confession has, in one sense, eclipsed 1 John as a whole and, in particular,
obscured the most seminal passage of the entire Epistle. I am referring
to the two verses in which the Apostle John frames a spiritual competency framework which depicts the journey into Christian maturity,
viz. a journey where we transform from being outer-persons driven by
our emotions to becoming inner-persons whom the Spirit leads. In this
journey, we pass through the key stages of life while achieving spiritual resonance – self-awareness, self-regulation and empathy. These
provide the platform for our being able to enrich and reproduce the life
of Christ in one another through authentic relationships.

1 John 2:12-14

> *I am writing to you, little children, because your sins are
> forgiven for His Name's sake.*

> *I am writing to you, fathers, because you know Him who is
> from the beginning.*

> *I am writing to you, young men[1], because you have overcome
> the evil one.*

> *I write to you, children, because you know the Father.*

1   Whilst the Apostle John uses the expression "young men" and "father", I see no
reason to suggest that this is an exclusively male designation.

I write to you, fathers, because you know Him who is from the beginning.

I write to you, young men, because you are strong and the word of God abides in you, and you have overcome the evil one.

In the passage, the Apostle John identifies three distinct groups of people, attributing to each group a set of characteristics. This book is the first in a trilogy based on these three groups of people and these groups will be referred to as "the three phases of the Christian life." In a nutshell, the Apostle John outlines for us the believer's often circuitous journey into oneness, circumscribing it thus – Little Children, Young Men and Fathers.

The Three Phases of Christian Maturity

1. Little children

"I am writing to you, little children, because your sins are forgiven for His Name's sake."

(1 John 2:12)

"I write to you, children, because you know the Father."

(1 John 2:13c)

Key Concept – Confidence

2. Young Men

"I am writing to you, young men, because you have over-come the evil one."

(1 John 2:13b)

"I write to you, young men, because you are strong, and

the word of God abides in you, and you have overcome the evil one."

(1 John 2:14b)

Key Concept – Competence

3. Fathers
Confident, conformed and confidants of God

"I am writing to you, fathers, because you know Him who is from the beginning."

(1 John 2:13a)

"I write to you, fathers, because you know Him who is from the beginning."

(1 John 2:14a)

Key Concept – Confidants

Each and every one of us has our own story to tell about the problem of Performance-Based Acceptance. For me, this problem used to be an acute addiction. It would take a large percentage of my life to stop obsessing over the question: Am I good? And will I ever be good enough? To finally come to the place of being able to reply: Why do you call (or wish to call) yourself good? Only God is good (Mark 10:18). Mine is a story about finding acceptance based on my identity in Christ alone without reference to works of any kind, good or bad. From the need for the approval of others to the realization that we are accepted in the Beloved (and more than simply being accepted, but also accepting of ourselves and others), this journey forms part of the first step along the road to wholeness. It is a knowing which comes through knowing who God is and who we are in His sight.

It might have been A.W. Tozer who said that the most important thing in the world is what you think of God. I would say that that is the second most important thing. The first is what He thinks of you. All of our problems as Christians stem from this one single issue. We have misconceptions of who God is, what He is like and what type of people He likes or dislikes. Most of us have only known the god of religion and he is no god at all. The God of the Bible is the God whose nature is *agapé* – unconditional, other-centred love.

I came to "faith" in 1987, but upon reflection the faith I had at that time was a faith in my faith in God. I had exhausted all my own financial and emotional resources. I was spent. At twenty-seven years of age I was undone. For reasons I would not bore you with here, I was a single-parent and raising four children under eight years' old. I was juggling my father-cum-mother role while trying to maintain a business and I was not doing very well in either of my occupations. I was anxious about the future, rueful about the past and clueless about the present. As it turned out, I entered the kingdom of heaven through the door marked "Pentecostalism". It seemed the right door at the right time. I took a seat and ordered a drink in what for me was the Last-Chance Saloon.

Through an unenviable set of circumstances which I would not have chosen for myself, I learned (in a "God meant it for good" way) that I was a helpless sinner, unable to save myself. In the paradigm of "Christianity" I entered into, though I was "saved", I had to learn another lesson which would take me fifteen full years to grasp. Previously, before I was "saved", I had not lived for God, nor did I want to do so. Now, I was desperately trying to live for God but could not do so. I learned the hard way, i.e., as much as I was once a helpless sinner, now I was a helpless saint. I would discover at length that true Christianity is not about imitation. It is about participation. For now, I was caught on the horns of a Romans 7 dilemma – the good that I wanted to do, I could not do. It is this realization that we cannot live for Him which will bring about our second great crisis of faith (i.e., crisis of faith in the self-life), leading us to the realisation that Christ is our life.

Summary of the Three Phases

LITTLE CHILDREN	YOUNG MEN	FATHERS
Cradle of Faith	School of Faith	Life of Faith
Conscious participation in His death	Conscious participation in His resurrection	Unconsciously conscious participation in His ascended life
The children know that their sins have been forgiven and they know the Father	From "milk" to "meat"; they have conquered the evil one; the Word of God abides in them	In-to-me-see (intimacy) with God who knows them (the fathers); oneness
Independent	Dependent	Interdependent
Main characteristic of the phase – Rest through self-recognition	Main characteristic of the phase – Recognition and self-regulation	Main characteristic of the phase – Reproduction
Jesus represents me before God – Intercessor	Jesus resides in me – Indweller	I represent God before men – Intercessor
Nature of perceived relationship with God –	Nature of perceived relationship with God –	Nature of perceived relationship with God –
Independent	Dependent	Interdependent
Pseudo-independence The illusion of separation	Realization of John 15:5 that "apart from (Him I) can do nothing."	Revelation of the mystery of Christ that He lives His life through us and we live our life through Him.
Discovering the Word of God through God's word, the Bible	The Word abiding in them — walking in the Spirit	Becoming the Living Word of God
External – For Christ	Internalizing – In Christ	Integrated – As Christ
Confidence in God	Competence from God	Confidants of God
Not Christ but I	Not I but I and Christ	No longer I but Christ
Forgiven	Forgiving	Redeeming/Reconciling
John 16:9	John 16:10-11	John 16:12
Convicted concerning sin and guilt	Convicted concerning righteousness and judgement	The "many (other) things"
Professing faith	Possessing faith	Possessed by His faith

Perhaps it is as well to start with a qualifying statement: Salvation is not accepting what He has done for you, it is receiving who He is in you (Romans 5:10-11). It is my experience that if I ask the average believer what they understand about the nature of their salvation, they will typically respond in terms of salvation being about getting out of hell and into heaven.

While that is true, it is hard to imagine a more impoverished view of the Christian life. Christianity is not so much about what happens to us when we die as it is about the revolution which occurs within us when we recognize the love of God.

Many of the people who have shared with me their experience of coming into contact with the Grace Message describe themselves as "being born-again-again"! It is a lovely expression and one which perfectly articulates the reason why I have given my time and energies to preaching what I call "The Gospel to the Saved". There can be no real spiritual growth without this experience and, in truth, we have to admit that much of what passes for spirituality in this day and age is, sadly, counterfeit.

So, how are we to define spiritual growth?

| "Spiritual growth" – an expanded awareness of what we already have and who we already are in Him.|

How does the Lord mature people?

All the evidence, both internally and externally, seems to suggest that all spiritual growth and progress is predicated upon the disillusionment with self-effort. Change occurs at the precipice, when we are staring into the abyss. Truly we must learn that just as He comforts the afflicted, He is not beyond afflicting the comfortable.

What is the role of the "Church" in this process?

I have begun to wonder whether the institutional "Church" ought to be viewed like the umbilical cord, where if the child were to become detached from it in the womb, the child would die, but should the child fail to be detached from the chord once it has been born, the child cannot live. Institutions should serve people but, unfortunately, it is often the other way around.

What is the deepest revelation which can belong to each phase
of growth?

I feel strongly that we have lost something of the Hebraic nature
of our walk with God. Our father was Abraham the Hebrew.

Scripture seems to point us to an understanding the Hebrew as
being someone who had crossed over, one who wandered from
place-to-place, a nomad who lived as an alien. The picture we have
is of a sojourner not a settler. I see him perhaps through romantic
eyes as one who, in the case of our Father Abraham, whilst he may
have started out seeking to obtain a physical inheritance, soon realized that the greater 'prize' was a spiritual inheritance. ⟶ *God's gift*

I feel that in our day we have reversed that journey; having
started out seeking a spiritual inheritance we have become distracted and have begun to seek merely a physical one. That is one
of the central themes of *The Intercessor*, the final book in this
trilogy so let me park the thought for now. Let us return to more
immediate matters:

The Little Child *(self-recognition)*
The summit of the Lord's disclosure to the Little Child is that
He has enabled the Child to become settled in the wonderful
truth that God is *for* him. He knows his Father and that his sins
(past, present and future) have been forgiven. Consequently, he
has peace with God and knows that nothing can separate him
from God's unconditional love for him. This phase will require
a profound renewal of the mind and deep repentance which will
result in a fixed change of the child's perception of who God is.
The revelation that God is love (1 John 4:8) does not come easily
to wary believers who have been conditioned to believe that they
are the ones who better have some good news to tell God rather
than allowing Him to tell them the Good News about His Son.
So busy is he rehearsing his prodigal's "I am no longer worthy"
speech (Luke 15:19) that he can't hear the Father saying, "Son,
we're throwing a party in your honour."

The Young Man *(self-regulation)*

This is the believer's pubescent period. It is characterized by the believer's recognition and self-regulation and thus, developing a spiritual competency framework. God has prepared works for him and he must be prepared for them. This is the phase I call "The Taming of the True" or "The Adapting of the Adopted". In plain language, it is a period of character development. The adolescent is enrolled into the *School of Faith*, readied for the *Life of Faith*. The believers will sit at the same desk and wander in the same deserts as the great men and women of faith have done. They will be tutored by the Law until Christ is fully formed in them (Galatians 4:19). There, they will undertake the same programme of self-awareness which has helped Jacob become Israel, Simon become Peter and Saul become Paul. There too, they will learn life's most profound lesson that *"the righteous shall live by His faith"* (Habakkuk 2:4) and that it is *"no longer I who live, but Christ who lives in me"* (Galatians 2:20).

I am certain that, as with its natural counterpart, this transitory period is the most awkward phase of the Christian life. Whilst the adolescent knows that nothing can separate him from the love of God, there is altogether too much of the self in him to connect him to the life of God. He knows that he is blessed but he is not yet a blessing. He is aware that there is no condemnation for him, but is beginning to also see that there is no commendation for him either. It is unlikely that he has yet failed enough to convince him of the wisdom of letting-go and letting-God. He must accept that once he was a helpless sinner and now he is a helpless saint. He must learn the mystery of the Vine and the workings of the D-vine. The summit of this phase is to fully integrate "Christ in me" into himself and manifest the deepest work of the Holy Spirit which is "self-control." All life in the Spirit is about letting-go. Self-control; not being in control; hardly, but rather getting the self under control in order that we might finally give up control.

The Father *(Reproduction and the nurturing of the nature of Christ in others)*
He has arrived at the summit of the Christian experience this side of heaven. The Apostle Paul wrote that there are ten thousand instructors but not many fathers. The father does not merely know Christ *in* him but also knows Christ *as him*. This is a truly mystical phase, one explored and expanded upon by the Apostle John in his writings. It is to these writings which we will turn in the final part of the trilogy. The father enjoys a supernatural cosmic harmony. Thus, the summit of the father's experience is one of unconscious competence – he does not know what he does know. He simply is!

The Four Levels of Competence:

4. Unconsciously incompetent – We do not know what we do not know.

5. Consciously incompetent – We know what we do not know.

6. Consciously competent – We know what we know.

7. Unconsciously competent – We do not know what we do know – we have become one with it.

His revelation is "Christ *is* me". However, critically, it is not that he is Christ but that he is fully possessed by Christ, so much so that he has become synonymous with Christ. He is not a god apart from Christ but is a part of Christ (Exodus 4:16; see also 1 Samuel 3:19-4:1). He no longer simply has faith in God; he now is said to have the faith of God (Matthew 21:21). This is the same level of faith which was operational in Moses (Exodus 14). Thus, the summit of this experience is intercession. This group, which the Apostle John identifies as "fathers", the Apostle Paul calls "you who are spiritual" (Galatians 6:1).

At the Father Phase we are expressers of God's nature. We stand as proof of His existence. We reveal His presence. We are His manifestation. We are Him materialized. We are no longer concerned with receiving the life of Christ; our one pre-occupation is to reproduce the life of Christ in others.

Hence, the Apostle Paul asserts that if anyone is in Christ, not only is he a new creation but also the old things have passed away and the new has come. But more than that, we ...

1. ... have been given the ministry of reconciliation \

2. ... have been entrusted with the message of reconciliation |

3. ... are ambassadors for Christ |

4. ... are the vessels through whom God makes His appeal |

5. ... implore men on behalf of Christ to be reconciled to God |

CHAPTER 7

THE CHILD PHASE

As stated earlier, the extent of a Child's understanding is that he[2] knows the Father and he knows that his sins have been forgiven. Prior to his being saved, he was not conscious of his need for a saviour but the Spirit convicted him of this need and thus, he sets out on the first stage of the Christian life. Having seen his condition, he accepts God's solution and receives His life. He no longer considers himself a sinner but reckons himself reconciled, redeemed and righteous, his sins having been both forgiven and forgotten. This is a very great advance as he has matured from his pre-rebirth position (where his core conviction was that he was not a sinner in need of grace – John 16:9), to being convicted of his unbelief in Jesus, to his post-rebirth condition of realising that he is the beneficiary of covenantal grace and thus he already was, is and ever will be forgiven. And now, having accepted his own forgiveness, he forgives (Ephesians 4:32). Furthermore, he is persuaded that he will be wrong to think of his sins as being forgiven by any means other than Jesus.

At this infancy stage the Child has only realized that the death of Christ has dealt with his sins. He has not come to understand that he is not saved by the death of Christ but by the life of Christ.

---

2 Throughout this book, unless otherwise stated, references to "he", "his", "son" and "men" include "she", "her", "daughter" and "woman".

have to discover

60

SAFE AND SOUND

Bad

If His death has dealt with sins (the fruit), His resurrection has
dealt with sin (the root). The child has not discovered his inner-
strength that will one day work so powerfully within him. While
the child is convicted of his unbelief, he has yet to be convicted (at
an experiential level) of his righteousness (John 16:10) or concerning judgement (John 16:11).

⟶▷ It is not uncommon for a new believer to unwittingly swap
unrighteousness for self-righteousness. In truth, pride attaches
itself so readily to the infant in Christ. It is pride that causes him
to seek to establish his own righteousness and it is pride that lights
the spark of judgment in him. Because he is not yet strong and has
not seen fully that the Word of God abides in him, he is susceptible
to and capable of being tossed to and fro by every wind of doctrine. Moreover, he is still unconscious of his Christ-righteousness
(John 16:11; 2 Corinthians 5:21). He can be overcome by his circumstances and has yet to be settled in his role as an overcomer
(Revelation 12:11). Whilst he knows the Father, he only knows
▷His acts and not His ways (Psalm 103:7-8). The child does not
even aspire to such a level of intimacy. For him, the milk stage is
sufficient, nourishing and wholly satisfying. He is not yet ready
for the meat which will be his staple diet in the second phase. Far
too many Christian re-births are ectopic (developing outside the
womb). The blunt truth is that the fertilized spirit cannot be located
anywhere other than in the uterus of grace and not in the fallopian
tubes of Legalism.

At this point it is worth raising a disturbing thought – if the
Apostle John is right where the definition of a Child is that "he
knows that his sins have been forgiven", how many Christians
know that their sins *have been* forgiven? To push the point further,
how many Christians are able to believe that even the sins which
they have not yet committed have in fact, already been forgiven?
In a recent television interview, I asked the host how many Christian leaders he knew who believed that *all* their sins, past, present
and future, had been forgiven? He hesitated before admitting that

very few, if any, knew this truth. Pressing him one stage further, I asked him how he felt about the "Church" being led by people who, according to a biblical standard, had not even reached the maturity of a child? Suffice it to say that his response betrayed his tremendous personal integrity.

We graduate from this Child phase when we are no longer "carnal Christians" and this is evidenced when our defining characteristic is that we are for others. We derive meaning, purpose and fulfilment from loving others and not just loving ourselves. It is when we become the following that we may be considered "safe sons":

◊ Self-givers, not self-getters

◊ Gratifying others, not self-gratifying

◊ Others-centred, not self-centred

◊ Others-serving, not self-serving

◊ Givers and receivers, not buyers and sellers.

It will benefit us to maintain a clear distinction between "saved sons" and "safe sons". Whenever we function out of self-protection or self-interest, we cannot, in all conscience, say that we are living as safe sons. In any event, whilst a believer may not be a safe son in the Child phase, he is still a *son*. That never changes. Even though he may behave contrary to who he really is, he is, nonetheless, still 100% a *son*.

As mentioned earlier, I have four children – Chantelle, Louisa, Francesca and Paul. From the very day they were born they were *100%* Chantelle, Louisa, Francesca and Paul, but they were just babies, knowing nothing whatsoever except who their parents were. They did not know who they were and they lived in complete dependence on an external relationship with their parents for their survival.

Taking Louisa for our example, let us imagine that as she began to grow up, she became more self-aware and instead of asking herself, "Who is Louisa? What do I want to be?," she asked herself, "How can I be Louisa?" That would be a non-question because *she is Louisa*. However, her journey will be to discover herself and find out who she really is. child phase

So, to recapitulate, we as little children know that our sins are forgiven on account of His name and that we know the Father. We will remain on the breast of doctrine until these two issues are cemented and we become strong. All God is to us at this point is what He is externally. We have yet to discover the consciousness of our hidden resources. We are yet to realize what has happened in us.

The Little Child …

… is unaware that God has blessed him with every spiritual blessing in the heavenly places in Christ.

… is oblivious to the fact that he has been chosen in Him before the foundation of the world and that he is holy and blameless before Him.

Child Phase	Teenager Phase	Father Phase
Conviction concerning our sins. Verdict – we do not simply believe in God; we actually believe God.	Conviction concerning righteousness. Verdict – we recognise that by grace, we are (not will be but *are*) as righteous as Jesus.	Conviction concerning judgement. Verdict – we recognise that we will judge the world.
Saved.	Sanctified.	Saviours.
No condemnation.	More than conquerors.	Just as He is, so are we in this world.
Elementary level.	Intermediate level	Advanced level.

... does not know that God has predestined him to adoption as a son through Jesus Christ.

... has yet to have the mystery of God's will fully revealed in him.

... does not know that he has obtained an inheritance and has not recognized that he is sealed in Christ with the Holy Spirit.

... does not yet know the hope of His calling.

... knows nothing of the riches of the glory of His inheritance in the saints.

... has not awoken to the knowledge of the surpassing greatness of God's power towards those who believe.

These are some of the things which the Child has yet to appropriate and will not do so until he enters the "Young Man" phase. However, this does not mean that the Child is not already His. The Child is. It is just that he has yet to realize it. My prayer for you, as we journey together in this book trilogy, is that you, dear reader, come to see that you too have been made alive in Christ. Whilst you were dead in your trespasses and sins, you have now been raised up with Him and seated with Him in the heavenly places in Christ Jesus.

May the words of the Apostle Paul pertain to us all in these days:

"That according to the riches of His glory He may grant you to be strengthened with power through His Spirit in your inner being, so that Christ may dwell in your hearts through faith – that you, being rooted and grounded in love, may have strength to comprehend with all the saints what is the breadth and length and height and depth, and to know the

*love of Christ that surpasses knowledge, that you may be
filled with all the fullness of God."*

(Ephesians 3:16-19)

CHAPTER 8

THE PARABLE OF
THE TALENT(ED)S

Matthew 25:14-30 – Seeing With Innocent Eyes
Most Christians (and that might well include you, dear reader)
may have been brainwashed into believing, as "truth", certain lies
about the nature of God which have negatively impacted the way
in which we relate to Him.

The Apostle John's choice of characteristics used to describe
the Child is illuminating. As noted earlier, according to the Apostle
John, the Child knows two things which are crucial to his wellbeing
– firstly, he knows that his sins have been forgiven and secondly,
he knows the Father.

Let us start by asking why these two characteristics are elementary truths. Is it that they are simply the most obvious points? Or is
it that without this knowledge and the want of it, it is obvious that
the Child's growth will be spiritually stunted. (For a fuller discussion of this subject see my book *The Bonsai Conspiracy*). I submit
that it is the latter.

The Child Phase can be summarized in one word – Assurance.
In the absence of assurance, the Child will inevitably develop self-
defeating behaviours. These behaviours, though designed to win

the performance trap

him the love and acceptance he so craves and without which he
cannot function healthily, will entrench in him a sense of anxiety
rather than enhance a sense of wellbeing.

That is why the Child's revelation must begin here. Quite simply, if the Child is not free to fail, he is not free to succeed. Nothing
on earth kills creativity like the fear of failure. So, love must do
its perfect work and cast out fear because he who fears cannot
be perfected in love (1 John 4:18b). The fact that our sins (past,
present and future) have been forgiven liberates us not only from
the penalty of sin, but also from its power which the Apostle Paul
tells us is in the Law.

Now, in John's gospel, the apostle quotes Jesus in the six-
teenth chapter, anticipating the dawning of the new age of the
Spirit, and informs his disciples that when the Spirit comes, He
will convict the world concerning sin, righteousness and judgement (John 16:8-11). Recall also that the Apostle Paul begins his
much-loved eighth chapter of Romans with this emphatic proclamation: *"There is therefore now no condemnation for those who
are in Christ."*

In order for us to make spiritual progress we must begin here.
Growing in grace is a bit like arithmetic. If you make an error in
the sum, you cannot just keep on going in the hope that the fault
will correct itself. It will not. You must go back to the beginning
and find the mistake. For most Christians, we need look no further
than here in the Child Phase. Almost without exception the error
lies with our mental map, i.e., our view of God. Until that view
and the accompanying underlying assumptions about Him are corrected, we will never feel either safe or sound.

There is an interesting exercise used in change-management
training to illustrate the problem of fixed or rigid thinking. It
is concerned with illustrating the potential problem with what
are called our mental maps. For these maps to be of value, they
need to be constantly updated. Imagine that you are a visitor
to London and are relying on a map from Victorian England

to help you get around the city today. It would not be of much help, would it?

The exercise consists of showing an image of what can only be described as a splash of ink randomly poured on a page. The delegates are asked what they can see. The answer is that they cannot make out anything coherent and thus, they are congratulated for viewing the image with "innocent eyes". Then, they are warned that in a moment, their view of the image will be fixed. The next thing which happens is that from the nothingness, an outline of a cow emerges. The delegates are exposed to the image of the cow for no more than two seconds. The cow quickly disappears and they are left staring at the "ink spill" again. The final and most alarming part of the exercise is that the delegates are invited to try and "unsee" the cow, which they find they cannot. That is because the image of the cow has now been indelibly etched on their minds, even after only a momentary exposure. The learning point is fascinating. If we become fixed in our thinking after but a moment's exposure to something, what happens when we are exposed to something all of our lives? We find that it is almost impossible for us to see anything else.

I want to suggest that for most of us, our mental religious maps are in dire need of updating. You and I live under the New Covenant of grace, not the Old Covenant of Law. We live under the self-regulating rule of God and not according to a set of rules, supposedly from God, to which my adherence will qualify me for God's acceptance. And yet, it is highly likely that most of us have been exposed to the Law (rules) for so long that we have become fixed and cannot see what we were before the Law or what we are after it. Nowhere is this more acutely felt than in the area of Bible reading. For many of us, the ink spill of our innocence has long since been replaced by the sacred cows of Legalism. For us to be able to read the Bible innocently again, it would take nothing short of a revolution. Actually, it would require what the Bible calls the *renewing of our mind* (Romans 12:2).

Perhaps you might think that I am overstating the case. Thus, let me invite you to read a parable with which you are likely to be very familiar and when you have done so, I wonder whether it will be possible for you to see it with "innocent eyes" or whether your religious map has spoilt the innocence and thereby fixed your paradigm forever?

As Keynes once put it:

"The problem lies not so much in developing new ideas as it does escaping from the old ones."

Matthew 25:14-30

For it will be like a man going on a journey, who called his servants and entrusted to them his property. To one he gave five talents, to another two, to another one, to each according to his ability. Then he went away. He who had received the five talents went at once and traded with them and he made five talents more. So also he who had the two talents made two talents more. But he who had received the one talent went and dug in the ground and hid his master's money.

Now after a long time the master of those servants came and settled accounts with them. And he who had received the five talents came forward, bringing five talents more, saying, "Master, you delivered to me five talents; here I have made five talents more." His master said to him, "Well done, good and faithful servant. You have been faithful over a little; I will set you over much. Enter into the joy of your master." And he also who had the two talents came forward, saying, "Master, you delivered to me two talents; here I have made two talents more." His master said to him, "Well done, good and faithful servant. You have been faithful over a little; I will set you over much. Enter into the joy of your master."

He also who had received the one talent came forward, saying, "Master, I knew you to be a hard man, reaping where you did not sow, and gathering where you scattered no seed, so I was afraid, and I went and hid your talent in the ground. Here you have what is yours." But his master answered him, "You wicked and slothful servant! You knew that I reap where I have not sown and gather where I scattered no seed. Then you ought to have invested my money with the bankers, and at my coming I should have received what was my own with interest. So take the talent from him and give it to him who has the ten talents. For to everyone who has will more be given, and he will have an abundance. But from the one who has not, even what he has will be taken away. And cast the worthless servant into the outer darkness. In that place there will be weeping and gnashing of teeth."

Take a few moments to summarize the key elements of this parable.

1. Having read the passage, how does it make you feel? Remember that I am not asking you for your *thoughts* on the passage at this stage but rather just how it has made you *feel*. What is your emotional response? (e.g., I feel happy, sad, anxious, light, frustrated or the like). *flustered, yet a feeling of not understanding.*

2. For you, what stands out the most about the passage? *that the man with one talent thought he was cruel. But he kinda seemed to be*

3. Does the passage seem to have any relevance to you in your walk with God? *yes, a little.*

4. With which character do you most readily identify? *the one with one talent*

5. How does the lesson apply to your life?

6. In view of the conclusions you have arrived at, what do you feel at this point? What is your intuitive response to God?

I suspect that most of us will be able to identify with the wasteful servant and find ourselves very much at home in his world. I can still remember the first time I heard a sermon on this parable.

I vividly remember the procession of feelings which washed over me – first anxiety and then guilt, followed by the resolve that I was *going to make something out of my life for God.* Like many new Christians, I should have been rechristened with the Scandinavian name, "Gunnar" because I was gunnar pray more, gunnar read the Bible more, gunnar go to Bible school, gunnar change for God. All these, you may say, are not bad things, but the truth is that what fuelled this urgent sense of commitment and dedication was fear and not faith.

I'm a gunnar

Reflecting on those early days when I "got serious with God", dedication and determination were such a feature of my life with Him. It is hardly surprising that before too long I suffered burnout and my brand of Christianity was found wanting. Over the last few years I have gone through a radical process of repentance and no, it is not the kind which you are thinking of. This is a repentance involving my changing my perspective of God and changing it so radically that He is now the God of the Bible and not the God of the "Christian religion". He is love and His perfect love has driven out all my fears.

As I read this parable afresh through eyes that have been given back their innocence, I wonder if the story really ought to be renamed as "The Parable of the Talented".

Let us look at the story again. Jesus says that our Father gives gifts (talents) freely and He gives them *gratis* and in His loving giving of the gifts there is neither the explicit nor implicit edict that by receiving the gift, the recipient is drinking from the poisoned chalice of performance. There is not the slightest whiff of the recipient being responsible for making something happen. In fact, the literal Greek word here for "giving" is "delivered". All the parable is saying is that the master gave the talents into the hands of the servants to (in Genesis style) keep, manage and take care of, together with the power to use the said talents (Genesis 1:28-30). The imposition of responsibility is imputed by the so-called "wicked" servant and not by the master nor by the other servants. Unsurprisingly,

the parable turns on the interaction between the "wicked" servant and his master. The first two accounts of the other servants
pass by without controversy, but the final account stumbles and
becomes the scene of a conflict between the master and his errant
servant. However, I want to suggest that the dispute happens for
reasons other than what our old outdated religious maps might lead
us to believe.

To my mind, this story is about how we are either loosed or
bound by our perceptions, about being freed versus frozen and
about risk aversion versus creativity. What transpires is, therefore,
not a reward/rebuke piece in response to the various individu-
als' powers of multiplication or commercial prowess, but rather
a reminder that God is the cause of His own effect and we are
"containers" and "conduits" of His divine life and energy. In short,
we are the manifestors of His nature. However, all too often, we
"contain" or, more precisely, "constipate" His life in us. Thus, we
become A-Dam rather than Adam who functions normally beyond
sin, failure and self-consciousness; Adam who names all the ani-
mals, has effortless dominion over all which has been delivered to
him and who enjoys the spontaneous multiplying life of Christ.

The first two servants present themselves, saying, "Look.
You've planted seed in us and it bore fruit from us." To which,
the master replies knowingly, "Well done, my good and faithful
servants. You've understood the divine economy." Both interviews
are unremarkable. This is because they view their master as being
loving and accepting. However, the rebuke, when it comes, is
reserved for the servant who sees his master as being capricious
and hard to please. The errant servant is typical of all of us who
insist on reading the Scriptures through the spectacles of the Law,
casting the Lord in the role of the misanthropic Ebenezer Scrooge
and us in the role of the put-upon Bob Cratchit. In this world,
the Lord appears as the Scrooge-like auditor of the universe who
keeps scores and demands usury rates of interest on talents which
we treat like a hire-car – we are terrified to drive it lest we have an

accident and lose our deposit. Such a vision of God does little to engender free-spirited creativity.

I think it is important to note that the "wicked" servant does not do anything which could be construed as an act of wickedness in the conventional sense of the word. What he has done, he does because he is afraid of God. Fear, having cast out perfect love in his mind, triggers a logical response: "You'd better not screw up. If you know what's good for you, you'd better play it safe because there'll be hell to pay if you waste your talent." The inevitable paralysis ensues. The servant's strategy is, therefore, consistent with his toxic perception of his master. In truth, what is evil is really altered knowing, i.e., perverted knowledge. Let us remind ourselves of the servant's description of his master:

> *"I knew you to be a hard man, reaping where you did not sow, and gathering where you scattered no seed, so I was afraid, and I went and hid your talent in the ground. Here you have what is yours."*
>
> (Matthew 25:24-25)

Note the emphatic description, "I knew you to be a hard man ….". He sees the master as harsh, rough, stiff, stern, violent, rough, offensive and intolerant and consequently, suffers from an acute fear of failure. This perception, unsurprisingly, makes him anxious. Continuing to project his own perception of his master onto the situation, he goes on to give First Adam's speech, almost verbatim: "I was afraid and I went and hid your talent in the ground, covering it up so that it would go undiscovered." Then, the servant throws his talent back at his master and says, "I don't want your talents. It's too much of a responsibility for me to bear. I'm not as gifted as the others. They're ten and five times more gifted than I am. They're your favourites. I'm just Cinderella without a fairy-godmother. I can't do it justice! I'll screw it up! I'm not good at that sort of thing! Here, you have what's yours. I don't want it, I didn't ask for it, I don't need it and in any case, I'm just a slave. Leave me that way!" c\osed off

His fear has blinded him from the mystery of grace! Certainly, he cannot even begin to grasp the principle that grace does its own work, that God is the cause of His own effect and that all He does is to invite us to co-operate with Him by trusting Him and letting His river flow out of our bellies.

The servant thinks that the onus is on him to produce. He must deliver. Yet, even though he thinks he needs to succeed, he is paralyzed by fear. For him, winning is defined as "not losing" and hence, he buries the talent in the ground, thereby inviting the rebuke from the master.

In truth, the Master is not concerned about the rate of return. He couldn't care less whether the effect of the flow of life from us is a hundred-fold or fifty-fold (which is the way the principle of the sower works). What matters is that the seed is scattered, the lamp is not hidden under a bushel and in this case, the talents are enjoyed and not buried. What the parable is patently not saying is that God is grading us on our works. 7,

As with a similar story in the Gospel of Luke, we see once again that to those who have much, more will be given and to those who have little, even the little which they have will be taken away. This is simply because until we understand God through the mystery of grace in all its outrageousness and all its absurdity, even the fingertip hold we have on the mystery will be lost. However, when we understand that it is all of grace, our grip becomes firmer and firmer.

So with the above in mind, let us consider the two characteristics that define child-level faith.

CHAPTER 9

YOU KNOW YOUR SINS
HAVE BEEN FORGIVEN

I know God loves me *but...*

As we saw in the previous chapter sometimes we simply cannot
un-see certain things. We get stuck in a mental groove and each time
we play the record the needle of our subconcious hermeneutic (the
interpretation of Scriptures) makes the impression slightly deeper
and evermore indelible. It is for that reason that I have often argued
that the biggest problem for learners is not what we don't know
about the Bible but rather what we think we do know. Nowhere is the
point more clearly made than in dealing with the question of forgiveness. Most of us know that we are forgiven yet that doesn't seem to
prevent us from seeking forgiveness and what is more curious even
fewer of us experience any discomfort living with the contradiction.

For the average modern Christian, asking God for daily forgiveness is as natural as brushing our teeth. We do it at least twice a
day and if truly dedicated to spiritual hygiene, we even floss after
every meal.

I can't help wondering that if we were to stop and think about it
we would see the conflict. You see we are forgiven. Full stop. Forgiveness is something that has been permanently acquired for us, it
is not something that is required by us. To this end we as believers

75

must be careful not to confuse the legitimate need to confess our sins (something we ought to do) with *our need* to ask God to forgive our sins to God (something we need not do). As Christians we do confess our sins but rather than asking God to forgive them we ought to thank God that He had forgiven them even before they had been committed. It is the very realisation that we are forgiven that gives us the confidence to confess our sins.

If during these last twenty years I have managed to grasp anything of the mystery of grace, it is the better-ness of the New Covenant (which is incidently a *covenant* and not a contract. A contract is an exchange of promises for the breach of which the law will provide a remedy).

In contrast to a contract, a covenant is a one-way agreement (whereby the covenanter is the only party bound by the promise). It is to conclude that to continually ask God for forgiveness having been forgiven is to:

> *"[spurn] the Son of God, and [profane] the blood of the covenant by which [one was] sanctified, and [outrage] the spirit of grace"*

(Hebrews10:29)

Now, of course, those who might query the unconditional nature of God's love will, no doubt, submit Hebrews 10:29 into evidence. Yet this evidence is clearly inadmissible. To expect the New Covenant to give evidence against the unconditional love, forgiveness and acceptance of God is to ask the Bible to perjure itself.

You, the jury, are invited to note the context of Hebrews 10:29. The writer to the Hebrews prefaces the verse by saying,

> *"For if we go on sinning deliberately after receiving the knowledge of the truth, there no longer remains a sacrifice for sins...."*

(Hebrews 10:26)

Hold on ... let us just look at that for a moment. Okay, if we go on sinning (I will come back to what this might mean in a moment) after receiving the knowledge of the truth, there no longer remains a sacrifice for sins.

Q: First off, what is the "knowledge of the truth" that we have received?
A: It is that Jesus died for the sins of the world and by that one sacrifice, He has made us forever perfect.

So, after having received, if we go on deliberately sinning (I am coming to that in a moment, no need to panic!), there no longer remains a sacrifice for sins. Err ... why not? Well, because the only suitable sacrifice for sins (i.e., Jesus) has already been made. There is and will not be any need for any more sacrifice. Nothing else. Not the blood of bulls and goats. Nothing. Thus, if you have received the truth and go on sinning, there is nothing else to know. Jesus is it. Full stop.
Alright then, what is sinning? Let us cut to the chase.

Q: How does Jesus define "sin" in John 16:8-9?
A: Unbelief: *"And when He comes, He will convict the world concerning sin and righteousness and judgment: concerning sin, because they do not believe in Me ...."* (John 16:8-9).

Q: When John the Baptist calls Jesus "the Lamb of God", what does he say that Jesus has come to do with our sin?
A: Jesus has come to take away the sin of the world (John 1:29)!

Q: What does "take away" mean?
A: It means "to remove" something. This is a vital point to note because under the Old Covenant, the people's sins were atoned for (i.e., covered up), but the word "atone(ment)" is never used

in the New Testament; the word "propitiation" (i.e., satisfac-
tion) is used instead.

Q: To use a modern illustration, when the garbage collectors
come, what do you want them to do with your rubbish? Atone
for it (i.e., cover it up) or take it away?
A: Well, of course, we want the rubbish taken away. That is why
the Bible tells us that as far as the East is from the West, so far
are our transgressions removed from us.

Q: What is the only way to remove the indelible stain of sin?
A: *"Indeed, under the Law almost everything is purified with
blood, and without the shedding of blood there is no forgiveness of sins."*

(Hebrews 9:22)

Nothing other than the shed blood of Jesus is sufficient to dis-
lodge the sin nature (the root) and remove the stain of sins (the
fruits). The shedding of His blood once and for all is deemed sufficient. One either accepts that fact (Jesus has done it all) by faith
or refuses to place one's trust in the finished work of the cross
and thus condemns oneself to a lifetime of uncertainty. Failure to
accept this (already received) truth renders the believers/doubters
haunted by *"a fearful expectation of judgement, and a fury of fire
that will consume the adversaries"* (Hebrews 10:27) which the
believers/doubters assume to be their lot if they do not meet and
maintain standards.

However, if one could but see, even His "judgement" is illusory
and presumed. Note the choice of words used by the writer to the
Hebrews: *"How much worse punishment, do you think, will be
deserved by the one who has spurned the Son of God, and has
profaned the blood of the covenant by which he was sanctified, and
has outraged the Spirit of grace?"* (Hebrews 10:29) Absolutely, the
punishment is deserved but the principle of grace is that we do not

get what we deserve; *au contraire*, what we get is precisely what we do not deserve. We deserve *punishment* but we get *presents*. We deserve *condemnation* but we get *commendation*. The believer is God's ambassador and not His adversary; His envoy and not His enemy. As we have seen, there is no punishment in love. I need to wave away your protests: "Surely," you may demand, "people who do such things cannot be in Christ? These people have turned their backs on Him!" Be that as it may, the truth is that He cannot not be in them and neither has He turned His back on them. That, in the end, is the only thing which counts.

Thus, to lay claim to child-level faith, the believer must believe and have grasped the most liberating of truths – Christians do not get forgiven; they *are* forgiven. In this chapter, I propose to examine this statement and hopefully, to both anticipate and answer any raised objections.

A couple of quick diagnostic questions to see if you are still with me:

Q: According to Ephesians 2:8-9, how did we get saved?
A: By grace through faith, wholly apart from works so that none might boast.

Q: Okay, having been saved, how are we expected to continue our Christian life according to Colossians 2:6?
A: "Therefore, as you received Christ Jesus the Lord, so walk in Him."

Let us stay in question and answer mode for a bit longer...

Reflective Questions

Text	Reflective Questions	Answer Suggestions
"In Him we have redemption through His blood, the forgiveness of our sins, according to the riches of His grace that He lavished upon us with all wisdom and insight." (Ephesians 1:7-8)	1. According to these two verses, what do we have in Him? 2. Since you are redeemed (bought back from slavery), how many times have you asked God to redeem you again? 3. Why would you ask for what you already have? 4. Did He redeem and forgive us without having the benefit of foreknowledge?	1. Redemption and forgiveness of sins. 2. My guess is none; which kind of begs the question, "Then why do we ask Him to forgive me every day?" 3. You would not unless you do not know that you already have it. 4. Not at all. That is the scary part. He redeemed us in the full knowledge that we would screw it up.
"He entered once for all into the holy places, not by means of the blood of goats and calves but by means of His own blood, thus securing an eternal redemption." (Hebrews 9:12)	Given that the word "eternal" means "without beginning and end, that which always has been and always will be" and the word "redemption" means "deliverance especially from the penalty of sin", can you see that you are free from both the power and the penalty of sin?	
"For by a single offering He has perfected for all time those who are being sanctified." (Hebrews 10:14) (Note that the word "perfect" here means "to make complete, to accomplish, to finish, to bring to an end".)	For how long and by what means have you been made perfect?	Always and forever; and by one ultimate divine sacrifice.

Text	Reflective Questions	Answer Suggestions
"For Christ died for sins once and for all, the righteous for the unrighteous, to bring you to God. He was put to death in the flesh but made alive by the Spirit." (1 Peter 3:18; NIV)	Based on this verse, what do you understand about the efficacy of the sacrifice of Jesus?	He died for us all once and for all and there is no distinction in the benefits of that sacrifice between the "lost" and the "saved". He gave His all and demands nothing at all.
"Then He adds, 'I will remember their sins and their lawless deeds no more. Where there is forgiveness of these, there is no longer any offering for sin.'" (Hebrews 10:17-18) (The literal translation of "forgiveness" is "remission" which means "release from bondage or imprisonment; the letting them go as if they have never been committed.")	How many of your sins can the Lord recall to His mind? What could possibly lead you to conclude that this pardon covers only pre-salvation sins when *none* of your sins had been committed at the time of the cross?	
"He does not deal with us according to our sins, nor repay us according to our iniquities. For as high as the heavens are above the earth, so great is His steadfast love toward those who fear Him; as far as the east is from the west, so far does He remove our transgressions from us." (Psalm 103:10-12)	If He does not deal with us according to our sins (i.e., our getting what we deserve), how does He deal with us? What has He done with our sins?	He deals with us according to His steadfast love. He has removed our sins from us.

Text	Reflective Questions	Answer Suggestions
"Behold, it was for my welfare that I had great bitterness; but in love You have delivered my life from the pit of destruction, for You have cast all my sins behind Your back." (Isaiah 38:17)	Why do you think that God has placed your sins behind His back?	Because God loves us. He has already dealt with our sins which He has seen the back of so that it be not an obstacle between us and Him.
"But as it is, He has appeared once for all at the end of the ages to put away sin by the sacrifice of Himself." (Hebrews 9:26b)	Who did Jesus appear for?	Jesus appeared for everybody which includes the entire population of the world.
"So Christ, having been offered once to bear the sins of many, will appear a second time, not to deal with sin but to save those who are eagerly waiting for Him." (Hebrews 9:28)	Why would Jesus not deal with the issue of sin at His second coming?	Because He has already dealt with it and from his perspective, it is a non-issue.
"And by that will we have been sanctified through the offering of the body of Jesus Christ once for all." (Hebrews 10:10)	How are we sanctified?	Through the death of Jesus.
"For our sake He made Him to be sin who knew no sin, so that in Him we might become the righteousness of God." (2 Corinthians 5:21)	Why did God make Jesus to be sin?	So as to make us the righteousness of God.

Text	Reflective Questions	Answer Suggestions
"For if, because of one man's trespass, death reigned through that one man, much more will those who receive the abundance of grace and the free gift of righteousness reign in life through the one man Jesus Christ." (Romans 5:17)	1. If you have received the gift of abundant grace, whose righteousness have you received and in whose righteousness are you standing? 2. Is there any unrighteousness or sin in God? 3. If you are in Christ, how much unrighteousness is in you?	1. In the righteousness of Jesus. 2. Of course not! 3. None at all.
"And you, who were dead in your trespasses and the uncircumcision of your flesh, God made alive together with Him, having forgiven us all our trespasses, by cancelling the record of debt that stood against us with its legal demands. This He set aside, nailing it to the cross." (Colossians 2:13-14)	When and how did God achieve this for us?	When we were dead in our sins. He achieved this when He cancelled the debt.

These verses seem to present a pretty compelling case. However, I am well aware that many of you will be thinking to yourselves, "Ah, but what about 1 John 1:9: *'If we confess our sins, He is faithful and just to forgive us our sins and to cleanse us from all unrighteousness'*?"

Before we discuss that verse, let me invite you to re-read the reflective questions, meditate on the quoted verses and then, ask yourself this one question: "In view of what I have just read, is it possible that the Apostle John intends this one verse (1 John 1:9) to completely negate the cross of Christ?"

I appreciate that the above might be a little melodramatic, but in truth that is precisely what is at stake here. To believe that the Christian needs to be forgiven is to:

> *"nullify the grace of God, for if righteousness were through the Law, then Christ died for no purpose."*
>
> (Galatians 2:21)

Let me put it to you in another way – what do you think happened at the cross?

Option A: Did Jesus die for the past, present and future sins of the whole world and having done so, did He deposit forgiveness in a heavenly bank account and give us the access security code of "1 John 1:9" which we can use any time we need to make a forgiveness withdrawal to pay off our debt?

Or,

Option B: Did Jesus pay off the debts once and for all – once and for all so that there is now no sin debt outstanding for anyone anywhere?

So, let us look at 1 John 1:9 with innocent eyes... and in doing so let me remind ourselves that if you are a Christian reading this book then we can assert with some confidence that you have already confessed your sins and at that time He who is faithful and just cleansed you from all unrighteousness; once and for all time. Nonetheless, in evangelical circles, the general approach to this verse goes something like the following:

"1 John 1:9 is not a verse applicable to the Christian"

Evangelical Objections	Grace Responses
Christians ought to be ready at all times to acknowledge any failure which God's light may expose to them.	I agree but what has that got to do with asking for forgiveness? Would it not be more consistent to acknowledge any such failure (confession) and then, instead of asking God for forgiveness, thank Him that despite our failure, we *are* forgiven?
The Apostle John's thoughts might be paraphrased as follows: "If we confess our sins, He *will* forgive the sins which we confess and moreover, He *will* even cleanse us from all unrighteousness."	What happens to the sins which we do not confess? The word "will" is future tense. Is the Bible not clear that this righteous act has already been granted (past perfect tense)?
There is no need to agonize over sins of which one is unaware.	Since when did ignorance become a defence? Even if that were to be the case, would amnesia not be the most desirable gift of the Spirit?
Christian fellowship with God is inseparably connected with "familial" forgiveness, i.e., Christians who never ask for their Heavenly Father's forgiveness prove themselves to be insensitive and thus, grieve Him.	In view of what the Bible says about forgiveness, do you not think it is more likely that the opposite is true? God has reconciled Himself to us. All that remains is for us to reconcile ourselves to Him.
The Lord's Prayer is a clear mandate instructing us to ask for forgiveness (Matthew 6:11-12).	Under what covenant was Jesus speaking when He gave the Lord's prayer? Do you think that under the New Covenant, if we do not forgive, God will not forgive us (even though He has made it abundantly clear that we are forgiven)? In Ephesians 4:32 the Apostle Paul places the issue of reciprocal forgiveness in the New Covenant era – just as you have been forgiven, so forgive. Is that verse not the New Covenant equivalent of the Lord's Prayer? (Note that it is not "… so forgive or else" but "… so forgive because you have already been forgiven.")

"If we confess our sins, He is faithful and just to forgive us our sins and to cleanse us from all unrighteousness."

At the risk of being overly simplistic, are we to understand that if we do not confess our sins, He will neither forgive nor cleanse us, even though we are already forgiven and cleansed? It is worth reminding ourselves that divine forgiveness does not require human assent for it to be operative. Divine forgiveness is not like a credit card where upon receiving it, you have to call the issuing company to activate the card. When Jesus cried from the cross, "Father, forgive them," nobody was recorded as saying, "Yes, Father, forgive me." They were already forgiven, plain and simple. It is the function of the cross to cleanse us of all unrighteousness and it is the consequence of receiving His life which made us righteous. Confession has no place here.

Furthermore, if the Apostle John is talking to believers, why, then, after having given us 1 John 1:9, would he pause and turn to another group (the group which is his primary audience) and say, *"My dear children, I write this to you so that you will not sin. But if anybody does sin, we have One who speaks to the Father in our defence – Jesus Christ, the Righteous One"* (1 John 2:1 NIV). I simply cannot see how 1 John 1:9 can ever apply to a believer in the way it is currently (mis)applied. However, the verse clearly does have an application and so, who is the Apostle John talking to?

One of the most common mistakes we can make when reading the Bible is to presume that everything written pertains to him or her. The entire Bible is true, but the *entire* Bible does not apply to you.

It may surprise some of you to learn that there are only seven letters in the Bible which are written exclusively to Christians. These are the so-called Prison Epistles (Ephesians, Colossians, Philemon and Philippians) and the Pastoral Epistles (1 and 2 Timothy and Titus, which were all written to the Apostle Paul's church-planters). Note that the Apostle Paul prefaced his Prison Epistles with greetings to the saints and faithful brothers. All the other letters were written to the church which was made up of the lost and the saved just as it is today. Moreover, none of the epistles were written in a vacuum but were, invariably, written in response to matters arising in the churches.

It is pretty well agreed that the letters 1, 2 and 3 John were written by the Apostle John, the author of John's Gospel, and it is interesting to note the similarities between the opening verses of John's Gospel and those of 1 John. The reason for the Apostle John's first epistle is stated in 1 John 5:13: *"I write these things to you who believe in the name of the Son of God that you may know that you have eternal life."* It is a message of assurance. Note that the purpose of John's Gospel is stated in John 20:31: *"But these are written so that you may believe that Jesus is the Christ, the Son of God, and that by believing you may have life in His name."* Thus, John's Gospel was written to *arouse faith* (so that one might believe) whilst his first epistle was written to *establish certainty* (so that having believed, one might go on believing and deepen one's belief).

Dating 1 John is a little unclear. However, scholars generally agree that it would have been written between the middle of to the last third of the First Century. By that time a number of things had happened – the separation of the Church and the synagogue was complete; the controversy over the issue of justification by faith had been resolved; the influx into the Church of the Gentile converts, with their heritage and philosophical thought, was beginning to inform the doctrines in the Church. The Gentile converts arrived with questions. They wanted to understand who Christ really was and thus were especially burdened by soteriological (what Jesus did) and Christological (who Jesus was) issues, e.g., "If Jesus was God, how could He die?" and "If Jesus did die, how could He have been God?"

Among the throngs of people drawn to the honey pot of grace, there was a particularly divisive group known as the Gnostics.

The church in Ephesus, which the Apostle John was addressing in his first epistle, had been greatly disturbed by the teachings of the Gnostics. In the Gnostic construct, salvation consisted of an escape from physical matter into the realm of the spirit. The chief means of effecting such an escape was to gain knowledge by which Man could, allegedly, rise above earth-bound limitations into a heavenly apprehension of truth. In a perverse twist, rather than being seen as the deceived and the sinner, Adam and Eve are perceived as being seekers of knowledge. I suspect that you can see where I am going with this, right? So, in that upside-down Gnostic world, the serpent is the good guy in the Garden of Eden and the Lord is cast as the bad guy. This is because the key to liberating Man from the bondage of God is to eat from the Tree of Knowledge.

However, of immediate significance and one which informs the Apostle John's first epistle is the central tenet of the Gnostic teaching – the doctrine of dualism. Dualism is the division of matter and spirit. The Gnostics consider all matter as evil and all spirit as good. Consequently, what one does with one's body is of no occasion. The Gnostics consider the human spirit as being trapped in the physical body, much like a pearl is trapped in an oyster. Yet, the spirit is part of the ultimate spiritual reality. This entrapment is thought of as being either "sleep" or "ignorance", but not sin, and for the human spirit to find salvation, it must be awakened and delivered from its ignorance by the recovering of knowledge of its true self as part of God. For the spirit to be saved, God has sent a redeemer to bring knowledge to the entrapped human spirit, thereby bringing illumination and salvation.

Intriguingly, the majority of Christian Gnostics identified that Redeemer as Jesus Christ. However, the Gnostics were generally docetic (i.e., "to seem to be") and thus they had resolved the Jesus dilemma by the ingenious suggestion that He only seemed to be human, but in reality He was not flesh and blood because if

He was, He would be disqualified from being God. In the second book of the *Until Christ Is Formed* trilogy entitled *The Apprentice*, there is a chapter called *The Silencing of Satan* which explains why Jesus had to be a Perfect Man. Jesus, the Last Adam, had to succeed where His predecessor, First Adam, had failed.

Self-evidently, if matter was evil and God was pure and if Jesus was really deity, He could not have anything to do with evil matter and therefore, the Gnostics reasoned that either 1. Christ was not really human and He only seemed to be so, or 2. the Christ Spirit did not actually inhabit the human Jesus until the baptism and left Him before His death on the Cross. The acceding to either option would have been fatal. The Gnostics advanced a view called Cerinthian which painted Jesus as being a sort of Jekyll and Hyde. Enter the Johannine epistles which were written to a pastor struggling against the tide of these heresies which were threatening to sweep the church away. Note the concerned tone in which the Apostle John wrote ...

◊ "Children, it is the last hour [for the community]"

(1 John 2:18)

◊ He refers to "deceivers" and "liars" who twist the truth

(1 John 2:19-26)

◊ These deceivers boast that they are "free from sin"

(1 John 1:8-10)

◊ They boast that they "have fellowship" with God but walk in darkness

(1 John 1:6)

◊ They boast that they "know God" but, nevertheless, are disobedient

(1 John 2:4)

◊ They boast that they are in the light but hate their fellow
brothers and sisters

(1 John 4:20)

Against this backdrop, and also reading this passage through the
lens of what the New Covenant as a whole says about forgiveness cf., John 19:30; Acts 10:43; Ephesians 1:7; Romans 4:7;
Colossians 1:14; Colossians 2:13; Colossians 3:3; Hebrews 9:22;
Hebrews 10:4; Hebrews 10:17-18:1; John 2:1-2, it ought to at least
raise a flag in our minds to ask the question: "Now that I am a
Christian, does this statement (1 John 1:9) still apply to me?"

Quite apart from the fact that we know that we are forgiven
surely any exegesis (an explanation or critical interpretation of a
Bible passage) would benefit from the commentator being aware of
the Gnostic problem that had surfaced in the church at that time.

As I have already suggested, the general epistles were written to
an eclectic group comprising of insiders, outsiders, off-siders and
off-the-wall-ers, and often included corrective content. It seems
likely to me that rather than instructing the believers in these opening ten verses, John is clearing the doctrinal decks by rebuking the
Gnostic group who were polluting the community with their lawless heresy; I choose the word 'lawless' carefully, as I want to draw
the distinction in your mind between 'lawless' and 'law-free'.

That, it seems to me, is the context into which we can find the
original (and intended) significance of the apostle John's opening
remarks. Ironically, the original significance has been buried under
the rubble of several hundred years of evangelical tradition in the
soil of which has grown this mixture of lore and grace.

The lore(s) has taken root in us. This particular folklore has
been granted especial hospitality amongst Christians who feel that
they need to ask for God to forgive them whenever they feel the
consciousness of their sins.

Of course some will argue that whilst we don't need to be forgiven per se, 1 John 1:9 nonetheless helps us in our walk with God.

Now I understand (and respect) why one might think that but, I want us to tread carefully here. If, we follow this logic then what we are saying is that whilst 'invoking' 1 John 1:9 doesn't affect our state of forgiveness but it does make us feel better, then are we not dangerously close to saying that 1 John 1:9 is in fact a placebo (a sugar pill)?

If that is correct then the question becomes: is it an innocuous form of spiritual medication? My feeling is that far from being inert, this may be a gos-pill with side-effects. I fear that long-term use can impair our spiritual insight, afflicting us with a myopia that renders us incapable of seeing the victory of the cross when we are distant.

If, as I am proposing, the way that we typically apply 1 John 1:9 is as a lore, and that is for you to decide, then it is to the New Covenant what the oral traditions were to the Old Covenant – an obstacle to intimacy. In Jesus' day these oral traditions (or fence-laws as they were also known) were afforded the same status as the Torah. Much of the conflict between Jesus and the Pharisees occurs because Jesus seems to play so fast-and-loose with these traditions. The Sabbath disputes are the text book example of this. The fence-laws were introduced to 'protect' the Torah (the commandments), however this insurance became so obsessive and burdensome that by the time Jesus arrived on the scene there were some 1500 oral laws surrounding the one law about the Sabbath cf., Luke 6.

Jesus had little if no respect for these traditions of men and his apparent contempt for them proved to be a useful device for drawing the fire of the Pharisees. Upon the canvass of their ire he would write large the mystery of the New Covenant that He had come to inaugurate.

I appreciate that writing on this subject is risky and I don't mind if having thought it through you should choose to reject it. Like all teachers I ask only for a hearing but if you reject it then at least know why you do. Don't let yourself be like the woman who used to cut the end of the ham. You probably know her story very well. But if you don't then permit me to tell it to you:

> There was a lady who, week-after-week, when she would pre-pare the Sunday lunch, which always consisted of a side of ham, would religiously follow her ritual of cutting the end of ham off of it. When questioned by her husband as to why she did that she replied: "We've always done our ham this way. My mother used to do it and she showed me." The husband was curious. He couldn't for the life of him understand why she would discard 25% of the ham week after week. So he went to his mother-in-law and asked her. She thought about it for a while and then replied: "We've always done our ham this way. My mother used to do it and she showed me." Well now the man was really troubled and so he went to see her mother, who was living out her last days in a retirement home. When the man asked this frail old lady about the ham he fully expected her to give the same answer. Imagine his surprise when she said with a puzzled expression on her face: "Umm, I don't know, Dear. I used to cut the end of the ham because my oven was too small. I have no idea why they do it. I thought ovens were bigger these days.

Okay, try this on for size: if the Gnostic error was to be de-sensitized to the ramifications of sin, i.e., they did not believe the sins they had committed mattered, the equal and opposite Christian error evidenced by our religious praxis is to be de-sensitized to the full ramifications of what God accomplished for us in Christ with the result that we (as Christians) are in danger of treating the consequence of the cross as if it didn't matter.

For this fetal error not to become a fatal one we must recognize that our walk in Christ is conveyed on precisely the same basis as our rebirth in Christ. Sanctification (which is the process of becoming who we already are and being who we have been set apart to be) is not appropriated through a progressive rectification of our behaviour through repentance and requesting forgiveness, it is realized through a progressive recognition of our identity through revelation and thanksgiving.

Now, that brings us back to our earlier conversation on premise. We noted that if our premise was wrong then our findings would also be wrong. Let's consider the respective outcome based on the trajectories of law and grace in terms of taking us towards a goal of godliness.

The Premise for our walk in Christ	
Law & Lore (John 1:17)	Grace & Truth (John 1:17)
I must become sanctified	I am sanctified (Hebrews 10:14)
Nurture	Nature
Works	Faith
Doing	Being
Behave	Believe
Ethical/religious life	Eternal life
Self-effort (supernaturally)	Effortless effort (supernatural)
Making it happen	Letting it happen
Re-dedication	Revelation
Cognition	Recognition
Morality	Mystery
Calculation	Contemplation
Transactional	Transformational
Resuscitation	Death and Resurrection
For me to live is to live like Christ	For me to live is Christ
Childish	Childlike
Container	Content
Tree of the knowledge of Good & Evil	Tree of Life
Result: sanctimonious (self-righteous)	Result: sanctified (Christ-righteoused)

This brings us to the very heart of why grace is so disagreeable
to the human ego. Ego's default setting is to *E*dge *G*race *O*ut.
When the ego, the self, the religious mind, call it what you will,
is confronted with the finished work of the cross, it quickly gets
agitated, restless and distracted, because it feels that it should
and ought (its two favourite words) to be doing something. It is
compelled to justify and validate itself.

▷ Why is this so? Firstly, because it feels obligated and, second,
because it needs to take the credit and feels as though it has made a
telling contribution. And that's precisely why grace is so vexing to
the flesh. Grace is about letting it happen, whereas works is about
making it happen. We are saved by grace through faith wholly
apart from works that no man might boast. And from the ego's
perspective that is what makes grace unpalatable. The ego wants
and needs to compare and judge itself against others. It derives its
validation from being able to assign a value, either good or evil
to its activities. The ego wants to compare, contrast and rank its
efforts over and against others.

It has rightly been said that sin is primarily religious, and secondly ethical. I suggest that the ethical sin of gnosticism was to
under-realize the importance of confession whilst the religious
sin of modern-day Christianity may prove to be that we have
over-realized it.

Ethical sins are easy to adjudge as being evil and labelled as
acts of unrighteousness. Religious sins, on the other hand, the
sins of self-effort, are more subtle because they appear 'good',
but that often belies the fact that those acts are in fact religious
sins in that they are acts of self-righteousness. Sin is always
unbelief in action.

Whether those 'sins' are good or evil they are fruit from the
same tree: the tree of the knowledge of Good and Evil; and that is
bad. Both these flavours of sin have two things in common: firstly
they should be confessed (that is that the perpetrator should come
into agreement with God concerning that behaviour or belief) and

secondly, whether they do or they don't confess, those sins are nonetheless forgiven.

The almost unthinkable reality about grace is that men and women do not go to hell because of sin. They go to hell because of unbelief; they go to hell because they did not accept God's free gift of life in Christ. In the same way, although we as Christians are going to heaven, we often live in a 'hell' of sin and guilt for the same reason – unbelief.

What God accomplished for us in Christ has freed us for all time from the penalty of sin. We are forgiven. Full stop. Our recognition of that and our ability to resist the temptation to forge a link between confession and God's forgiveness in the life of a believer is what keeps us from the power of sin. For, as Paul told us, the sting of death is sin, and the power of sin is the law. 1 Corinthians 15:56.

Now whilst we will never be punished for our sins, we are inevitably castigated by them. His imputed righteousness has dealt once and for all our putrid acts of unrighteousness, that is our prone-to-wander-detours into who we once were as opposed to the pressing into who we are now (1 Corinthians 6:9-11). We can rest assured that we are safe and sound: "It is finished", our sins and lawless deeds He will remember no more.

Our accounts with God have been forever balanced by Christ's finished work on the cross. His righteousness stands as the one and only acceptable (and already accepted) sacrifice for sins. However, embracing the gospel means embracing one another and extending to each other the grace which we ourselves have freely and unconditionally recieved. Now this is where the subject of forgiveness becomes highly relevant.

It would be an odd spiritual mentor indeed who would counsel his or her protégé to withhold forgiveness until the offender had asked for absolution. For surely the mentor would know that the witholding of forgiveness plunges the withholder into an even more dreadful darkness rendering him unable to walk in the light.

The blunt truth is that, having been forgiven, our emphasis ought not to be on receiving forgiveness for ourselves, it ought properly to be on extending it to others. Interestingly, the medical profession seem satisfied that forgiveness is good for our mental health. It has been proven that encouraging forgiving attitudes and emotions leads to decreased anxiety and depression.

The price for our sins has been paid, but there remains a high price to pay for unforgiveness. There are both therapeutic and restorative reasons why we should forgive. In truth the forgiven are forgivers. This is the economy of grace:

"forgiving one another, just as God in Christ forgave you"
(Ephesians 4:32)

This is the pathway to the restoration of our relationships with one another and a healthy Christian life (James 5:16). More on this later but for now and in the light of the foregoing let's get back to the text:

1 John 1:1-10

"That which was from the beginning, which we have heard, which we have seen with our eyes, which we looked upon and have touched with our hands, concerning the word of life – the life was made manifest, and we have seen it, and testify to it and proclaim to you the eternal life, which was with the Father and was made manifest to us – that which we have seen and heard we proclaim also to you, so that you too may have fellowship with us; and indeed our fellowship is with the Father and with his Son Jesus Christ. And we are writing these things so that our joy may be complete. This is the message we have heard from Him and proclaim to you, that God is light, and in Him is no darkness at all. If we say we have fellowship with Him while we walk in darkness, we

*lie and do not practice the truth. But if we walk in the light,
as He is in the light, we have fellowship with one another,
and the blood of Jesus His Son cleanses us from all sin. If we
say we have no sin, we deceive ourselves, and the truth is not
in us. If we confess our sins, He is faithful and just to forgive
us our sins and to cleanse us from all unrighteousness. If we
say we have not sinned, we make Him a liar, and His word
is not in us."*

The Apostle John insists he has audible, visible and tangible testimony that Jesus has come in the flesh and is God.

"This life," the Apostle John says, "is revealed and we have
seen it and testify to it and we declare to you the eternal life that
is with the Father and is revealed to us." And then, the Apostle John extended an invitation to the Gnostics to believe, "We
declare to you what we have seen *so that you also may have fellowship with us*; and truly our fellowship is with the Father and
with His Son, Jesus Christ." What the Apostle John was saying
was that the Gnostics could have no Christian fellowship with
one another whilst these issues stood between them. Confronting
the brutal truth, the Apostle John continued, "Look, God is light
and in Him, there is no darkness at all. What does He say about
the Gnostic party who claims to have fellowship with Jesus and
yet walk in darkness? They lie and do not do what is true. This
we compare and contrast with the believers who walk in the light
as Christ is in the light. And it is with these believers and not the
Gnostic party whom we have fellowship with. However, if we ...
(the Greek word used here is the royal "we" which means "all of
us, everyone, you and me"; it is a very common teaching device
to speak associatively as though the "we" includes us which it
most certainly does not) ... confess our sins, He who is faithful
and just will forgive us our sins and cleanse us from all unrighteousness. If we say that we have not sinned, we make Him a liar
and His word is not in us."

Then, having clarified the situation of the interloping Gnostic party, the Apostle John drew a broad smile and one could almost hear his tone change,

> *"My little children, I am writing these things to you so that you may not sin. But if anyone does sin, we have an advocate with the Father, Jesus Christ the righteous. He is the propitiation for our sins, and not for ours only but also for the sins of the whole world."*
>
> (1 John 2:1-2)

To illustrate the point further, consider the Apostle John's acid test in a following later passage:

> *"Beloved, do not believe every spirit, but test the spirits to see whether they are from God, for many false prophets have gone out into the world. By this you know the Spirit of God:* ***every spirit that confesses that Jesus Christ has come in the flesh is from God, and every spirit that does not confess Jesus is not from God.*** *This is the spirit of the antichrist, which you heard was coming and now is in the world already."*
>
> (1 John 4:1-3)

It is clear to me, at least, that the Apostle John's concern was not to instruct the church in the way of asking God for daily forgiveness but rather to bring the Gnostic anti-Christs to heel and to salvation and the reception of forgiveness.

The Apostle John's purpose here in the fourth chapter was not to show the naïve young saints how to get forgiven, but how to protect themselves from interlopers. As the Apostle John's Second and Third Epistles confirmed, the dear saints at Ephesus had developed the unfortunate knack of welcoming those they should have guarded themselves against and of guarding themselves against those to whom they should have flung wide open the doors of hospitality. The Apostle John gave them a means of authenticating the visitors. "One simple diagnostic question will do," he said. "Ask them if they believe that Jesus, being God, came in the flesh. If they say no, they are not from God." It was an infallible way of dealing with the Gnostic peddlers. The Apostle John furnished them with the perfect means of dealing with door-stepping Gnostics.

The difference between the religious world view of our relationship with God and the true position can, by analogy, be seen as a contrast between dial-up internet and a high-speed broadband internet connection. God is always on-line and, in fact, we as believers are embedded into the Divine Server. This connection, this fellowship, cannot be broken.

What the Bible says about fellowship with God is none other than the fact that:

> *"[He] will sustain you to the end, guiltless in the day of our Lord Jesus Christ. God is faithful, by whom you were called into the fellowship of His Son, Jesus Christ our Lord."*
>
> (1 Corinthians 1:8-9)

The "If" Word

If this teaching is unfamiliar to you and yet you've been gracious enough to stay on the bus without the need to ring the bell and get off, then you still might have a nagging doubt about this vision of grace. And that doubt might relate to what I call the 'if' word problem.

Even if you know you don't need to ask forgiveness one could reasonably feel that it is nonetheless possible for us to break fellowship with Him. Well, if that were possible, and it is not, then it surely would not be because we do not ask for forgiveness but precisely because we keep on asking Him to forgive us repeatedly. How would you feel as a parent if, having made a promise to your children, you were bombarded by their constant asking of whether

you really mean it? Our insistence on placing obstacles and inter-
mediaries between God and Man has kept us from ever realizing
the fullness of love.

In his letter to the Colossian church, the Apostle Paul makes a
most enlightening statement on this subject:

> *"And you, who once were alienated and hostile in mind,*
> *doing evil deeds, He has now reconciled in His body of flesh*
> *by His death, in order to present you holy and blameless and*
> *above reproach before Him."*
>
> (Colossians 1:21-22)

Now, I would be the first to accept that we may not be vindicated in
either our own sight or in the sight of others, but from God's perspective there are no issues to be resolved. Then, the Apostle Paul
goes on to make a statement which, unsurprisingly, has fuelled a
tremendous amount of uncertainty amongst the religious community. He begins with, "If ..."

> *"If indeed you continue in the faith, stable and steadfast, not*
> *shifting from the hope of the gospel that you heard, which*
> *has been proclaimed in all creation under heaven ...."*
>
> (Colossians 1:23)

Now, unless the apostle is prepared to dig up the very ground
of assurance which he has spent his life establishing, he cannot
have intended us to hear the word "if" as a conditional clause
and indeed, he does not want us to hear that. What the Apostle Paul wants us to hear is not "if" but "inasmuch", "as" or
"since". Here is a prime example of just how we have been
taken hostage by the vagaries and prejudices of translators. In
the popular modern version of the Bible, the NIV, the translators take the same root word and translate it differently on
two separate occasions in the same letter. This is because the

translation reflects the translators' doctrinal bias as opposed to a logical translation of the original sense of the text.

Correct as to the best of my knowledge, see:
http://www.biblestudytools.com/Lexicons/Greek/
grk.cgi?number=1489&version=kjv

The word *"ei[ge"* in the original Greek is a conjunction and means "if", "indeed", "inasmuch", "as" or "since". There is also a second Greek word, *"eij,"*, which is a primary participle of conditionality and means "if" or "whether". The NIV translators translate **Colossians 1:23** and **3:1** thus:

Colossians 1:23 (NIV):
"If [ei(ge] you continue in your faith, established and firm, not moved from the hope held out in the gospel. This is the gospel that you heard and that has been proclaimed to every creature under heaven, and of which I, Paul, have become a servant."

Translation options available:
 if;
 indeed;
 inasmuch;
 as; or
 since.

Colossians 3:1 (NIV):
"Since [eij,], then, you have been raised with Christ, set your hearts on things above, where Christ is seated at the right hand of God."

Translation options available:
 if; or
 whether.

The above, I submit, is not logical. How can the word "since" be favoured in the translation of Colossians 3:1 when it is not even an available option, whilst on the other hand it is overlooked in Colossians 1:21 when it is a clear choice? The simple fact of the matter is that the key word in the texts which drives the interpretation is in our mind, i.e., our minds have been conditioned to interpret it in a certain way. God has never and will never alienate us. Repentance is always about changing our perspective. The nature of salvation is the alignment of our thoughts with His through the renewal of our minds.

CHAPTER 10

THE TRUTH ABOUT CONFESSION

Thus, you might ask, "Alright, I see where you're going but let me ask you: Are you saying that having been forgiven, Christians need never confess their sins again?"

I am glad you asked and the answer is an unequivocal, "No". However, let us be sure that we are clear on this. Jesus has taken the written code (the Law) which was against us and nailed it to the cross (Colossians 2:14). The Law brings wrath but where there is no Law, there is no violation (Romans 4:15). Christ is the end of the Law so that there may be righteousness for everyone who believes (Romans 10:4) which, incidentally, is why there is no condemnation for those who are in Christ (Romans 8:1).

Now herein lies the rub. The average Christian confesses his or her sins so as to get forgiveness. I want to respectfully suggest that this may be flawed logic since it is self-evident that forgiveness is based purely on the shed blood of Jesus and not on confession. Confession does, however, have an important role. The Greek word for "confess" is *homologeo* which means "to say the same thing as another, i.e., "to agree with, to give assent". It is simply agreeing with or saying the same thing as God. Now, at any moment when the Holy Spirit convicts us of some misalignment it is appropriate for us to "confess our sin", and that of course is what trips the 1 John 1:9 switch in our minds. But it is inappropriate for us to then overrun the base and ask for forgiveness again. It is simply a matter of thanking the Spirit for revealing our sin, thanking God that we are forgiven and then, to go on rejoicing.

God's method of dealing with His children is not to put them under guilt trips when they sin. *Au contraire.* As we have already suggested, it is the certain knowledge that the armistice has been declared which gives us the confidence to confess our sins. It is precisely because we are forgiven that we confess our sins. It is well to remember that salvation is not getting our sins forgiven and going to heaven when we die, but is about the profound realization of the love of God and the recognition that His life runs through our veins. Consequently, as we grow in grace, we begin to see that the real fruit and blessing of forgiveness is the compulsion to forgive. Just as nobody can withhold forgiveness without paying a price, nobody can release forgiveness without accruing the benefits of forgiving.

The Lord wants us to experience the joy of forgiving as much as He wants us to revel in the joy of being forgiven. He wants us to receive this truth in the depths of our hearts and let it govern our attitudes and our actions, both towards ourselves and towards others. Thus, says the Apostle Paul in his letter to the church in Ephesus (Ephesians 4:28-32), the link between confession and forgiveness relates to our human interactions and not to our divine interactions. When our human interactions are spoilt by self-love, the divine antidote is other-love which is also the balm of Gilead, possessing the power to heal, mend and restore fellowship within spiritual communities.

"Let no corrupting talk come out of your mouths, but only such as is good for building up, as fits the occasion, that it may give grace to those who hear. And do not grieve the Holy Spirit of God, by whom you were sealed for the day of redemption. Let all bitterness and wrath and anger and

*clamour and slander be put away from you, along with all
malice. Be kind to one another, tenderhearted, **forgiving one
another, as God in Christ forgave you.** "*

(Ephesians 4:29-32)

The Apostle James makes the very same point in his correspond-
ence (James 5:14-16):

*"Is anyone among you sick? Let him call for the elders of the
church, and let them pray over him, anointing him with oil
in the name of the Lord. And the prayer of faith will save the
one who is sick, and the Lord will raise him up. And if he has
committed sins, he will be forgiven. Therefore, confess your
sins to one another and pray for one another, that you may be
healed. The prayer of a righteous person has great power as
it is working. "*

In the Apostle James' letter, the emphasis is also the restoration
of horizontal relationships within the spiritual community. He
encourages the ecclesia to *"confess [their] sins to one another."*
They are to openly acknowledge the wrongs they have done to one
another so that their relationships would be restored and healed.

In summary, the biblical injunction is that just as we are forgiven, so we forgive (Ephesians 4:32) but this is, self-evidently, in
proportion to our faith as an individual, i.e., the degree to which
you realize that you have been forgiven, so forgive. Under the
Law, "forgive or you will not be forgiven". Under grace, "you are
forgiven and so, you can forgive; just as you have been accepted,
so accept" (see Romans 15:7). This, then, is freedom. This is what
restores fellowship. This is how the children of God live.

"When we nurse old grudges, refuse to forgive others and wilfully oppose the Spirit within, we become adversaries – not only
in our relationship to God and others but in our relationship to
ourselves as well. We undermine the very conditions of our own

happiness and in the end, make ourselves utterly miserable. It is as if we fling ourselves into the fiery pit. Only in this modern scientific age, perhaps, are we beginning to understand in full the devastating psychological consequences of refusing to forgive those who have wronged us."[3]

3   Thomas Talbott, *The Inescapable Love of God* Universal Publishers/ uPUBLISH.com 1999

CHAPTER 11

YOU KNOW THE FATHER

That we have been forgiven, *gratis*, of all our sins, past, present and future, is a truth beyond our immediate comprehension. The reason we have difficulty accepting such "child-truth" is because we do not really know what God is like. We have been told that there are certain people whom God likes and dislikes, and have been encouraged to cultivate types of behaviour that will please Him, but we do not know Him. We know about Him and have even seen His acts, but we do not know His ways.

And this is what makes the Apostle John's second characteristic of the Child Phase so interesting. The apostle simply and matter-of-factly says that the Little Child "knows the Father."

What do little children, who have the privilege of being raised in a healthy family environment, know about their father? I think the answer is simple – they love and trust their dad. Although they know only some details about their father (what he does, what his middle name is and such), that does not prevent them from trusting their father totally and unquestioningly.

When my children were growing up they followed a ritual which used to absolutely terrify me every evening when I came home from work. Regardless of what I might be carrying or doing, as soon as they heard my arrival, they would come flying out of their bedroom where they had been playing and hurl themselves

down the stairs screaming, "Daddy!" When I say "hurl" I really
mean *hurl* – they would literally fly through the air at me. They
took it for granted that I would catch them. I do not think it ever
occurred to them that I would not, after all, I was their Daddy. I can
tell you there was more than one occasion when I thought that their
confidence was misplaced. But that is never the case with God. Little wonder that the Lord should say to the disciples,

> *"Suffer little children to come unto me, and forbid them
> not ..."*
>
> (Matt. 19:14; Mark 10:14; Luke 18:16 KJV).

God can be trusted. We can place our confidence in Him because
of who He is.

I must tell you that my entire Christian experience changed
in an instant the very moment I *knew* the Father. I can say for
the first time in my life that I felt safe and sound. When I was
perusing 1 John 4:8 one day, I came across something that I
had read many times before, but it was as though I had seen it
for the first time in my life. And it stunned me. In the eighth
verse, the Apostle John makes this startling statement: *"God is
love."* Notice that he did not say, "God loves" but rather, "God
is Love". I knew from thereon that I would be unable to separate my understanding of God from my understanding of love.
If God is love, I thought, what then is love?

In my book, *The Bonsai Conspiracy*, there is a chapter entitled
What's Love Got To Do With It? which provides a full discussion
on this most critical statement – God is love. Nothing in my life
to date had prepared me to engage with the depth of this statement. The best I had known hitherto was a tainted self-love; an
agenda-stained love. Most of us are familiar with the brand of
love that effectively says to us, "I love you because I need you."
What we are to discover is a love that says, "I need you because I
love you."

There are only two words in the Bible where each word merits a chapter dedicated entirely to describing it: Faith (Hebrews 11) and Love (1 Corinthians 13). Faith is the revelation of the second phase of the Christian life (the "Young Man" phase), but love is the foundation without which all faith and all activity are worthless. The realisation that God is love ought to thrill our souls and cause us to soar, to run and not grow weary, to walk and not grow faint. Sadly, for some (if not all) of us, the concept of love causes us to hesitate. We are cautious of it, suspicious even. That, I would suggest, is due to our becoming more accustomed to the counterfeit rather than the real thing where experience triumphs over hope resulting in our tendency to withdraw, to be compulsive, inhibited, rejected, disdainful and to mistrust. These fear-inducing introjections have caused us to run from, and not run to, God.

Let us remind ourselves of the Apostle Paul's poetic definition of the nature of love.

"If I speak in the tongues of men and of angels, but have not love, I am a noisy gong or a clanging cymbal. And if I have prophetic powers, and understand all mysteries and all knowledge, and if I have all faith, so as to remove mountains, but have not love, I am nothing. If I give away all I have, and if I deliver up my body to be burned, but have not love, I gain nothing. Love is patient and kind; love does not envy or boast; it is not arrogant or rude. It does not insist on its own way; it is not irritable or resentful; it does not rejoice at wrongdoing, but rejoices with the truth. Love bears all things, believes all things, hopes all things, endures all things. Love never ends. As for prophecies, they will pass away; as for tongues, they will cease; as for knowledge, it will pass away. For we know in part and we prophesy in part, but when the perfect comes, the partial will pass away. When I was a child, I spoke like a child, I thought like a child, I reasoned like a child. When I became a man, I gave up childish

ways. For now we see in a mirror dimly, but then face to face.
Now I know in part; then I shall know fully, even as I have
been fully known. So now faith, hope, and love abide, these
three; but the greatest of these is love."

(1 Corinthians 13)

When the Apostle John wanted to ascribe a word to capture the
essence of what the Apostle Paul described as the nature of love,
he did not rely on the classical Greek words *phileo* and *eros*. To
the Apostle John these two were inadequate. In fact, *eros* would
become the antithesis of the word that he would use for love. *Eros*
is lust (self-love) and not other-love.

You'll be familiar with the image of Cupid who is depicted
with a bow and arrow. These arrows are the flaming darts of
the enemy for which we have the shield of faith to deflect the
sting. The word *eros* literally means, "I desire for myself the
highest and the best". So, instead of the *eros*, the apostle chose
an unused Greek word, *agapé* to convey his meaning. *Agapé*
means, "I desire for others the highest and the best". *Agapé* is
"me for others" and this *agapé* is as absurd as it is outrageous.
To the religious mind, it is risible but yet, it is the truth about
the God of the Christian Bible.

God is love and God loves us and His love is unconditional. To
love us is both His heart's desire and His fixed choice. *Agapé* finds
its meaning, purpose and fulfilment not in acquiring all it can for
itself, but in being all it is for others. It is in giving and not getting
that *agapé* finds its fulfilment.

I believe that the Apostle Paul (who is by his own admission
a master builder – 1 Corinthians 3:10), rather than pouring these
characteristics into a bowl like some pleasant smelling potpourri,
has in fact thoughtfully placed them in ascending order. Indeed,
each of the characteristics not only builds the profile of *agapé* but
equally importantly, completes, step by step, an ascent of Mount
Carmel until we finally arrive at the breathtaking summit.

Agapé
is patient
is kind
cannot envy
does not boast
is not proud
is not rude
is not self-seeking
is unprovokable
keeps no records of wrongs
thinks no evil
rejoices in the truth
bears all things
believes all things
always hopes
always perseveres
never fails

Because as a Child we "know the Father" and the Father is, in the essence of His Being, love, I want to spend the following chapters journeying together with the Apostle Paul through each of the characteristics of *agapé*. Through understanding these different facets of love we will come to a greater understanding of the nature of the Father and how He views each one of us.

I would ask you not to rush, but to take time to admire the view at each vantage point. To help you, I have provided a series of personal reflection questions at the end of each characteristic. Take time to ponder the questions and grasp the enormity of each staging post.

CHAPTER 12

AGAPÉ
IS PATIENT

It was not immediately apparent to me why the Apostle would think to start his ascent of the mountain with this characteristic until I realized how we use the word "patience" nowadays. I thought about the number of times I had heard the expression, "I'm losing my patience" when I was growing up or how many times I had both heard and said, "You're trying my patience." The more I thought about it, the more I realized what a profound effect the word "patience" had had on me during my formative years. With disturbing ease I was able to recall the anxiety I felt (and, to a much lesser extent, still feel) when someone was trying to explain something to me which I did not understand. Whenever they had lost me in the conversation I would have this terrible inner struggle about telling them that I did not get it, because I did not want them to lose patience with me. Many a time when someone gave me instructions, rather than seeking clarification, I would just nod like I understood. In my mind at least, I had forged a link between patience and acceptance/rejection. Patience was a kind of approval/disapproval barometer.

I have thought about my life struggle with instructions and it is like those demonic things which you get with self-assembly furniture. I can guarantee you that if I start working on something like it, I will "lose my patience" with it. Why? Well, it is simply because I do not have any love for things like that. Where there is no love, there is no patience, but where there is love and understanding, there is an indefatigable amount of patience.

Now, I want to make sure that we do not miss something very important here. Whilst it is right to say that we are patient with those we love, life and love are not quite so straightforward. There is no doubt that I love my children. However, I distinctly remember attempting to teach Chantelle how to read. It drove me absolutely crazy; it all but exasperated her in the process (I did not know about Ephesians 6:4 back then). I had wanted her, before she started school, to read the complete works of Shakespeare; well, not quite but you get my point. I am horrified now when I look back and think of the hours I sat her down with one of the broadsheet newspapers and got so frustrated when she did not get it. Now, how come I lost my patience with her if love is patient? The answer is simple but crucial. You see, I wanted her to be able to read for *my* benefit. I wanted her to be thought of at school as a genius because it would reflect well on me. That, my friend, is not love. Love wants nothing for itself. It has no agenda other than to love.

When people tell me they are being "patient with me", what I assume is that they actually want to beat the living daylights out of me, that they are effectively withholding their anger and thus, I should be careful not to push it too far. Consequently, in my previous religious paradigm, the god of that world would stay his anger towards me provided that I did not push him too far. I had not understood that "patience" is calm endurance of hardship, provocation or delay. It is tolerant forbearance born out of calm self-possessed waiting. "Patience" is, in fact, core to God's nature and is neither limited nor conditional. It simply is a description of His nature. God *is* patient and this is completely different from stating that God is *being* patient, which He is not. He is patient in disposition and not imposition. When I finally realized that God was not tutting the whole time and getting impatient with me because I did not get it, that liberated me. Despite my stupidity, He never lost His patience, never chided me and never thought about getting rid of me by replacing me with someone who would get it.

For a child, I can see how this understanding of patience is integral. I had taught four children how to walk and not once did I lose my patience with them nor write them off and say to them, "You're wasting my time, you'll never get it." Every attempt was celebrated. Indeed, the more they failed at walking, the more I cheered them on. Moreover, I knew that they would walk when they were ready and not before. All they got from me was the constant encouragement, "Yes, you can do it. I believe in you. I will show you how."

It is easy to see the value of knowing that *agapé* is patient because it means that *agapé* gives us room to fail without censoring us. It also means that we are freed to not get it and yet not be adjudged as being stupid. In short, it means that love is set in the context of assurance and, therefore, it is rooted in the ground of no condemnation. Patience gives us permission to fail and consequently, permission to succeed. As we always say at The Grace Project, "If you're not free not to do something, you're not free to do it either."

Q: How does the idea that God will never lose His patience with you make you feel?

CHAPTER 13

AGAPÉ
IS KIND

The Apostle Paul's next step is to say that love is kind. What then is kindness? Kindness is the quality of being warmhearted, considerate, humane and sympathetic. At the heart of kindness is a willingness to forgive. It is hardly surprising then that the Apostle Paul should place kindness as the second of the attributes of *agapé*. Because *agapé* is patient and it understands, *agapé* is thus sympathetic and forgiving.

Is it possible, I wonder, to define forgiveness more deeply than to say "their sins and lawless deeds I will remember no more"? When we are discipled by *agapé* we are loved enough to change. The generosity of kindness ensures that even correction can be embraced. What a problem we have in our generation with people who are unable to speak without offending people who are unable to listen without defending! *Agapé*'s kindness cuts through that so that speaking the truth in love, we might build one another up.

The German theologian and physician, Albert Schweitzer, once said, "Constant kindness can accomplish much. As the sun makes ice melt, kindness causes misunderstanding, mistrust and hostility to evaporate."

There can be few things more healing than kindness. It is easy to see why the apostle would place it next to patience in his portrait of love. Kindness is, in a very real sense, an extension of patience. Kindness goes to the very heart of Christian love because kindness is charity and, as the much loved comedian, the late Bob Hope, put it, "If you haven't any charity in your heart, you have the worst kind of heart trouble."

When writing to the church in Rome, the Apostle Paul would surely have raised the religious eyebrows by stating that it was this very characteristic of *agapé* which not only heals but also redeems.

> *"Or do you presume on the riches of His **kindness** and for-bearance and patience, not knowing that God's **kindness** is meant to lead to repentance?"*
>
> (Romans 2:4)

The fact that it is the kindness of God, and not His imagined unkind-ness, which leads us to repentance is hugely significant. However, that is why grace is so difficult for people to really embrace. Our concept of God has been framed by our view that He is a god of regulations and not relationships.

The View From Sinai	The View From Calvary
Anger	Calm
Enmity (hating)	Friendship (loving)
Fear	Confidence
Unkindness	Kindness

Many people intuitively feel that a fear of God's wrath is what causes us to repent. We have been programmed to think "repent or else" instead of "wow, what else can I do but change my mind concerning God in the face of His affection, altruism, benevolence, charity, courtesy, decency, forbearance, gentleness, good intention, goodness, good will, grace, helpfulness, hospitality, humanity, indulgence, patience, philanthropy, sweetness, sympathy, tenderness, thoughtfulness, tolerance, understanding, unselfishness?"

So, kindness is generosity and compassion. It is numbered among the seven virtues which are the opposites of the seven deadly sins.

The Seven Deadly Sins and Their Corresponding Virtues

Pride is the excessive belief in one's own abilities which interferes with one's recognition of the grace of God. It has been called the sin from which all the others arise. Pride is also known as Vanity.

Opposite = *Humility*

Envy is the desire for the traits, status, abilities or situation of others.

Opposite = *Kindness*

Gluttony is an inordinate desire to consume more than what one requires.

Opposite = Abstinence

Lust is an inordinate craving for the pleasures of the body.

Opposite = *Chastity*

Anger is manifested in the individual who spurns love and opts instead for fury. It is also known as *wrath*.

Opposite = *Patience*

Greed is the desire for material wealth or gain, ignoring the realm of the spiritual. It is also called *avarice* or *covetousness*.

Opposite = Liberality

Sloth is the avoidance of physical or spiritual work.

Opposite = *Diligence*

It is interesting to note that the corresponding sin to the virtue of kindness is envy, because the third characteristic of *agapé* is that it cannot envy. When one reflects on what envy is (a desire for what others have), it is easy to see why *agapé* cannot envy. *Agapé* is and can only ever add value to others; it can never take away value.

Kindness is recognized and esteemed by all cultures and religions. The Talmud claims that "deeds of kindness are equal in weight to all the commandments." In Buddhism one of the Ten Perfections (*Paramitas*) is *Mettā*, usually translated into English as "lovingkindness", which Christians recognize as the word for "grace". Tenzin Gyatso, the fourteenth Dalai Lama, wrote, "my religion is kindness."

Nobody in the world knows me better than my wife, Hayley. On a whim, I sometimes think to myself about how she reacts to my kind of "kindness" and quite often, though not always, her response is to say, "What are you after?" It is such merited cynicism which we must keep in mind when we think about God's kindness. The first thing to be absolutely clear on is this – for kindness to be *agapé* kindness it must want nothing for itself. That principle is non-negotiable. If kindness wants anything for itself it is disqualified. *Agapé* is always and can only be "me for others". It can never be "others for me". Kindness having anything up its sleeve is not kindness at all. It is manipulation or seduction. Sadly, the vast majority of our exposure to "kindness" has been the counterfeit variety which, in truth, is manipulation, i.e., self-giving in order to promote self-getting: "I give so I can get".

Agapé is kind. And, as with anything to do with *agapé*, it is kind because it is kind; not to gain any favour or advantage or to reciprocate, it is kind because it is kind. As the saying goes, "Treat everyone with politeness, even those who are rude to you, not because they are nice but because you are."

Q: How do you feel knowing that God is kind to you not because He wants something from you but because it is His nature?

CHAPTER 14

AGAPÉ
CANNOT ENVY

Since envy is the opposite of kindness, it follows seamlessly that if *agapé* is kind, it cannot envy. *"Does a spring pour forth from the same opening both fresh and salt water?"* (James 3:11). So, if God is one thing, He cannot also be something that is opposite.

According to the seven deadly sins, envy is the desire for the traits, status, abilities or situation of others. As such, *agapé*, which is "self-for-others", cannot envy. That is the kernel and central truth of *agapé*. It can only ever be "me for your benefit". Envy is the signature of the self-life. Envy is the desire to take from others, while *agapé* is the compulsion to give to others. Envy demands that "what is yours is mine" whereas *agapé* declares "what is mine is yours". *Agapé* gives all it has to us – for free.

All of us have felt envy's sting while some of us bear its scars, physical and emotional. Such wounds run deep and they run the deepest when the sting comes at the tail of "love". There will be very few of us who have not been the victims of envy and/or jealousy or who have never been envious or jealous of others.

If patience is giving others permission to fail, not being envious is giving other people permission to succeed even if that means leaving us behind. Gore Vidal's comment that "whenever

121

a friend succeeds, a little something in me dies" is uncomfortably close to the truth.

What is "envy"? It is the feeling of displeasure produced by witnessing or hearing of the advantage or prosperity of others. If allowed to take root, envy quickly and easily becomes jealousy. Jealousy is distinct from envy in that jealousy does not simply feel displeasure, but goes on to give birth to an indignation which desires to deprive the victim of that of which it is envious and take it for itself. In contrast, *agapé* is never jealous *of* you, it is jealous *for* you. *Agapé* loves people and uses things; it does not use people and love things.

> "A tranquil heart gives life to the flesh, but **envy** makes the bones rot."
>
> (Proverbs 14:30)

Q: How do you feel knowing that God is not jealous of you but is jealous for you, and that you will never need to be jealous ever again because part of His being jealous for you is that He is jealous on your behalf?

CHAPTER 15

AGAPÉ CANNOT BOAST

The reason why *agapé* cannot boast ought to be obvious: *agapé* is other-centred while boasting is fundamentally about self-glorification. Boasting lies at the heart of *eros* because it says, "Look at me, look how good I am!"

The boastful, like the envious, cannot help but interpret things that happen to them and others from the narrow perspective of what it means to them. However, *agapé* is for others. *Agapé* is always a turning away from self. It is not self-deprecation, but an appreciation of others; not a putting down of self so much as a lifting up of others; not boasting (which is "counter-intuitive" since the opposite of "boasting" is "humility") and not humiliation, but the lowering of self.

Agapé stoops. Because *agapé* is "me for others", it revolutionizes our interaction with others, giving us the ability and desire to listen. It also enables us to concentrate on *being interested* and not *being interesting*, to *be impressed* and not *be impressive*.

Q: How do you feel knowing that God never says, "Look how good I am", but instead, just boasts about how good you are?

123

CHAPTER 16

AGAPÉ
IS NOT PROUD

Nothing in our lives has prepared us to accept this statement as being even a possibility, let alone, a fact. It is intriguing that in modern day usage, the word "pride" is often employed to convey a very positive sentiment, but when I encounter that word in the Bible, almost without exception, every reference to "pride" is negative. It therefore presents me with something of a dilemma, because on this basis I want to say that God is proud, i.e., He is not ashamed of me and He is "proud" of me. Yet, love is not proud. Thus, what does the Apostle Paul mean when he says that *agapé* is not "proud"? Well, let us try and define the word "proud".

In modern usage, to say "love is not proud" is to say that "love has no shame". The lover is not beyond humiliating himself in lavish shows of affection for his loved one. Which of us who have studied the life of King David (described as being a man after God's own heart) is not captivated by the total lack of pride in his love for God? Perhaps it has escaped us that God is equally abandoned in His love of and for us.

Oh that we could only see how, when we are restored to Him, that He (like King David in 2 Samuel 6:14) also dances with all His might! And when frigid religious appropriateness rebukes us,

"You ought not make merry with such vulgar people!", oh that we also see how love answers that rebuke,

> *"I will make merry before the Lord. I will make myself yet more contemptible than this ... "*
>
> (2 Samuel 5:21b-22a)

To be "proud" is to feel greatly honoured or pleased. Herein lies the root of the problem and the reason why *agapé* cannot be proud. Pride is the hallmark of the self-life. Pride is the antithesis of *agapé* because pride makes the most extraordinary and appalling boast by saying, "I don't need your help; in fact, I don't need anything or anyone because I can make it on my own."

Symptoms of Pride in Everyday Life

◊ Pride is a refusal to be vulnerable

◊ Real men do not cry (Oh, really?)

◊ Why do men refuse to accept that they are lost and let their wives consult the map?

◊ Pride is a refusal to accept that we need help in one way or another

◊ We think that needing help makes us look weak

◊ Pride says, "I have no need of God."

> *"In the pride of his face, the wicked does not seek Him; all his thoughts are, 'There is no God'."*
>
> (Psalm 10:4)

There are few things more damaging or dangerous than pride. The great trouble with it and the reason why *agapé* can never indulge in it is because, as C.S. Lewis put it, "A proud man is always looking down on things and people; and, of course, as long as you're looking down, you can't see something that's above you." *Agapé* never looks down on people. It can only ever look up because, as we shall see later, *agapé* believes the best. Now, this is most important because when we treat people as they appear to be, we make them worse. But when we treat them as if they already are what they potentially could be, you make them who they really are.

Here is the most staggering thought: if *agapé* is not proud (which it is not) and pride says, "I have no need of you", the collision of these two statements means that *agapé* says, "I do need you." *Agapé* (God) needs us because He loves us unlike *eros* which loves us because it needs us.

Remember, *eros* says, "I love you because I need you." *Agapé* says, "I need you because I love you."

Q: How do you feel about the fact that God wants to be vulnerable with you and confide in you?

CHAPTER 17

AGAPÉ
IS NOT RUDE

Here is another seemingly innocuous agapé characteristic, but it is because we use the word "rude" in a very different way now than when the Apostle Paul used it in 1 Corinthians. There is one other reference to this word in his second letter to the church at Corinth:

> *"But though I be rude in speech, yet not in knowledge; but we have been throughly made manifest among you in all things."*
>
> (2 Corinthians 11:6; KJV)

Now, interestingly, various different translators have opted to translate the Greek equivalent of the word "rude" in different ways and in so doing have added some real richness to it. Both the NASV and the ESV translate the word as "unskilled". The Vine's Expository Dictionary provides an even further illumination by pointing to the word "ignorant" and this definition offers us an interesting and important perspective. The moment we say that *agapé* is not ignorant, we raise an important issue, because to be ignorant is to have want of knowledge or perception. The Jews were said to be "ignorant regarding Christ" (Acts 3:17) but can we say that Christ was ignorant concerning the Jews? The answer is, of course, no! The Apostle Paul says that the Gentiles were wilfully ignorant (i.e., blind) concerning God (Ephesians 4:18), but can we say that God was ignorant concerning them? Again, no!

The other helpful definition of the word "rude" is "coarse" meaning rough, unpolished or incomplete. Whilst we can say that Man is coarse, rough, unpolished or incomplete, can we say the same of God who has declared on the workbench of the cross, "It is finished!'"? Was He mistaken then? Did He not know the facts? Was He ignorant?

> *"He has perfect knowledge."*   (Job 37:16)

> *"He knows everything."*   (1 John 3:20)

Is God in for a rude awakening in that while He wills that none should perish, apparently many (if not, the vast majority) will? Were His calculations rude? Did He get His sums wrong when He risked it all on the cross? Was He ignorant when He said that *agapé* is patient, kind, does not envy, does not boast, is not proud, is not rude, is not self-seeking, is not easily provoked, keeps no records of wrongs, does not delight in evil, rejoices in the truth, always protects, always trusts, always hopes, always perseveres and never fails if the opposite were to be true?

Are we to believe that the Lord Himself is the Foolish Builder of Luke 14:28-30? Did God fail to calculate the true cost of saving us? Will He not be all and in all? Did His Son fail to reconcile all things and make all things subject to Himself? Is the Law of sin and death greater than the power of the Spirit of Life? Was Adam's trespass leading to death more powerful than God's gift of life (Romans 5:12-21)? No, of course not.

Q: What would be the consequence for you, personally, of believing that Jesus is not the Foolish Builder?

CHAPTER 18

AGAPÉ
IS NOT SELF-SEEKING

Nobody likes selfish people, so why would we want to worship a selfish God? Yet the impression I get from many people is that they see God as not only selfish, but egotistical. So, it is crucial that we ask ourselves, "What does it mean to say that *agapé* is not self-seeking?" The word "seek" means to make a search for, to inquire, to try or to want, to get, to ask for or to request. At another level, it means to single out for companionship. Yet, *agapé* cannot do all that for itself. It can only do them for others. It can only search for, inquire, try, want, get, ask, request, single out for companionship *for others*. Do you realize that the Bible rarely, if ever, speaks of receiving love? The experience of love is not when you receive it but when you give it.

A dear friend of mine, Mike Zenker, the director of Steve McVey's *Grace Walk Canada* coined a great phrase: "learning to live loved". It is a tremendous concept and an even greater challenge. If we are to begin to rise to it, we will do well to reflect on the fact that for love to love it can never require anything from that which is loved.

Q: How do you respond to the principle that God wants nothing from you?

CHAPTER 19

AGAPÉ
IS UNPROVOKABLE

Whenever I speak on the nature of God, people invariably find this characteristic the biggest single stumbling block. The very notion that agapé cannot be provoked is almost blasphemous.

I can immediately anticipate objections to this as you and I can find a number of biblical references to the Lord, apparently, being provoked. It is interesting how dictionaries attempt to define the word "provocation" as something which arouses a strong response from another. How many of us have ever heard the expression "grieving the Spirit" or heard someone say something like "the Spirit is sensitive"? What do you suppose those statements mean? I want to suggest that in the context of an *eros* god, they mean something radically different from what they mean in the paradigm of *agapé*. When I say that someone is sensitive, I could mean one of two things and both are opposites to each other.

"X is very sensitive about that sort of thing."
(in a negative sense)

With this statement, you might think that X is touchy or easily hurt and that you ought to be careful around X or be careful to avoid

certain subjects while making sure that you are on your best behaviour. As a result, you become cautious, disempowered and unlikely
to be yourself around the person.

"X is very sensitive." (in a positive sense)

Perhaps now you might think that X will be able to empathize
with you and be a good person to talk to about a specific subject
such that you could confide in them by being frank and candid,
knowing that you would not be judged. As a result, you would be
encouraged and empowered.

Now, let me ask which of you has not believed, either consciously or subconsciously, that the Holy Spirit is "sensitive" in
the negative sense of the word? Worse still, we have been taught
that we can provoke Him to either bless us or curse us and consequently the "Church" who are authors, perpetuators and sole
beneficiaries of this lie, strive to keep this deception alive and keep
us in fear of God and be under their control. In the anti-Christ
system which most of us have uncritically accepted as authentic,
the clearest implication is that provocation, like patience, has a
max-out point. The bottom line is that "provocation" means something which arouses action or activity; a readiness to retaliate at the
slightest prodding. The consequences of saying that *agapé* is not
provoked are seismic because we are saying that *agapé* is fixed (in
being other-centred). It cannot be moved, swayed or tossed to and
fro. It has already taken its stand and there it remains.

If God cannot be provoked, on the one hand He cannot control
you with the threat of punishment and on the other, you cannot
manipulate Him to profit from Him.

Q: Do you feel liberated by the idea that God cannot be provoked by you either positively or negatively?

CHAPTER 20

AGAPÉ KEEPS NO RECORD OF WRONGS

"Said one man to another, 'When my wife and I argue, she gets historical.'

His friend replied, 'Surely you mean she gets hysterical?'

'No,' his friend assured him. 'She gets historical!'"

—anonymous

Not so long ago I was invited to lecture on the subject of grace at a Bible school here in London where I was challenged by one of the students on what he considered to be the outrage of grace. Among the statements which infuriated him was this from 1 Corinthians 13. For him, it simply was a bridge too far since the supposed conclusion was nothing more than a licence to sin. He could not see that grace, rather than freeing us to sin, freed us *from* sin. To my incensed student, the insistence that God keeps no record of wrongs is to imply that grace amounts to a Sinner's Charter. Be that as it may, his comments do reveal that many of us, as Christians, are in a fatal love affair with the Law. We simply cannot leave the Law because we are addicted to keeping score of the infractions of others. As such, we allow ourselves to believe that everybody, especially God, is keeping score on us. It is simply ludicrous to suggest to the religious mind that because of the day of reconciliation (at the cross), there will never be a day of reckoning. I am not sure which of the following is the more intolerable thought to our legalistic minds:

1. We will not be judged for the wrongs we have done to God and others

or,

2. Others will get away scot-free with the wrongs they have done to us.

But, there it is. We get away with it all. Full stop. It was this final statement which broke the religious camel's back as my young student blurted out in violent protestations. "So, what motivation is there to live a holy life?" he demanded. Religion is such a strange concept, is it not? If we are to progress in our spiritual walk, we must reckon that Jesus did not simply die *for* our sins, He died *to* them as well.

> Q: How different would your life be if you really believe that God keeps no record of your wrongs and that He has pressed the delete button and erased the record from His memory of every sin, past, present and future?

CHAPTER 21

AGAPÉ
THINKS NO EVIL

Whilst self-evident, this statement of the characteristic of *agapé* is so much more profound than we might dare to even imagine. Take a moment to think where it is located. The Apostle Paul's choice of location in the progression is as significant as his choice of words to describe it:

> *Agapé* keeps no records of wrong
>> thinks no evil
>> rejoices not in iniquity but rejoices in the truth

Such is the subtlety of the Apostle Paul's point that I will try to unpack this statement expositionally, relying on the KJV with Strong's Numbers version of the New Testament.

> *"[Love] doth not behave itself unseemly, seeketh not her own, is not easily provoked, thinketh no evil ...."*

Let us take the phrase "thinketh no evil" word by word. The word "thinketh" means "to reckon or count". It is perfectly legitimate to translate the word as "to take into account" and this reckoning is an inward weighing up; to deliberate or judge. Then, the next word that the Apostle Paul used is "no". The meaning of "no" is "no", i.e., it is an absolute negative; none, absolutely none! So, when "evil" is added to the end of the phrase, we are about to make a statement which is simply unthinkable. For "evil" here means "a bad nature". It describes a thing not being what it ought to be and a mode of thinking, feeling or acting which *agapé* will not take into account. Thus, my own translation of this verse looks like this ...

The Anderson-Walsh Interpretation of 1 Corinthians 13:6a (based on the KJV with Strong's Numbers):

Agapé reckons, counts, attributes, infers, judges and weighs (contrary to our expectation) absolutely no evil whatsoever; be it an evil nature, error, thought, feeling or even any action or behaviour, be it base, wrong, wicked, troublesome, injurious, pernicious, destructive or baneful. *Agapé* reckons it not.

Q: How do you feel and what difference would it make to your daily walk if you accept as a fact that He sees no evil in you?

CHAPTER 22

AGAPÉ
REJOICES IN THE TRUTH

The definition of "rejoices" is: exults, triumphs, expresses great joy, glories in, is jubilant, feels happiness or joy, walks on air, on cloud nine, jumps for joy, ecstatic, wallows.

To describe the Lord God Almighty as the dancing God who rejoices over us with singing is, for many, a difficult concept to fit within our religious construct. Yet, He is indeed the Lord of the Dance and it is into that divine rhythmic movement that we have been enjoined. God is in the rejoicing business which is a delight to all but those predisposed to religion. Whilst this dance is a delight to Prodigals, it is an outrage to Elder Brothers. Who can ever forget the portrait of indignation which is the Elder Brother in the story of the Prodigal Son; how the Elder Brother froze in disbelief, turning quickly into fury, as he approached the house and heard the music and dancing (Luke 15:25)?

What great disservice has been done to the Lord and His children by those who have presented Him as the killjoy of the universe?! To so many it seems that John 15:5 has been mistranslated and should read as *"because of You, I can do **nothing.**"* Far from being a kill-joy, our Lord was *killed for the joy* set before Him (Hebrews 12:2) and yet, He is still perceived through the performance-tinted

spectacles of the Law as being the "bah-humbugging" Ebenezer
Scrooge of the universe with the "Church" who is cast in the role
of Bob Cratchit.

The Elder Brothers of this world, just like King David's wife,
Michal, have no interpretative grid for reckoning the Father as
being the God who will be even more undignified (2 Samuel 6)
than the father in the parable of the Prodigal Son. It is simply not
a concept on their radar. However, in these days, amidst the dirge
of religion, there are those of us who can hear the refrain of perichoresis[4], the sound of the dancing God.

Q: Would you like to join Him in the dance? What is stopping you?

4   Baxter Kruger, www.perichoresis.org. Perichoresis: "Genuine acceptance
removes fear and hiding, and creates freedom to know and be known. In this free-
dom arises a fellowship and sharing so honest and open and real that the persons
involved indwell one another. There is a union without loss of individual identity.
When one weeps, the other tastes the salt. It is only in the Triune relationship of
Father, Son and Spirit that personal relationship of this order exists, and the early
Church used the word 'perichoresis' to describe it. The good news is that Jesus
Christ has drawn us within this relationship and its fullness and life are to be played
out in each of us and all creation."

CHAPTER 23

AGAPÉ
BEARS ALL THINGS

Surely it would be remarkable to boast that *agapé* bears all things if we mean that *agapé* "endures" all things, or to put it in more contemporary language, "*agapé* puts up with all our nonsense." I remember when I first began to engage with the Calvinist teaching of the "perseverance of the saints", I could not help wondering if the real miracle was not that the saints persevered with God, but that God persevered with the saints. Of course, the blunt truth is that God perseveres with us regardless of our fidelity, but that is not what is on view here. There is a much deeper truth.

The Greek equivalent word for the verb "bear" is *stego* which means "to thatch or to cover". The idea conveyed is that "*stego*" seeks to preserve an object by covering and shielding it from harm, and protecting it from anything which threatens it.

While not an exact parallel, the imagery of "thatching" and "covering" evokes memories of Noah and his Ark. Indeed, that story captures the very heart of this most magnificent characteristic of *agapé*. Genesis 6:14-8:1 recount the story of Noah's Ark and record Noah's graduation from the school of faith to the life of faith. The Lord instructed him to make a boat and in so doing, provided him with meticulous specifications. Noah was told to "pitch" the boat inside and out (Genesis 6:14) and it is this word "pitch" which demands our attention. What is being crafted for us in this account of Noah is typological. The event is pointing towards the cross, illustrating in the natural realm what will happen in the spiritual realm. "To pitch" means "to cover, purge, make atonement or make reconciliation". It is derived from the Hebrew word *kaphar* which is "to cover over or to atone for one's sin; to propitiate".

Now, here is the really exciting part. You will recall that it was Noah's family who went into the Ark and there they found shelter from the storm and safe passage to dry land (the new earth, if you will). In the same way today, we, the believers, are placed into Christ (Colossians 3:3) in whom we find shelter from the storms. We are brought safely to the New Jerusalem and preserved from the impending judgment. Thus, the Ark is a type of Jesus. The purpose of the pitch was to make the Ark watertight. Indeed, we will see later in this book that our salvation is watertight. However, you may ask, "How could Noah and his precious cargo know that they were safe inside the Ark?" The answer is delightfully simple. They were safe because the Lord shut them in, sealing the outside of the Ark Himself.

*"And they that went in, went in male and female of all flesh, as God had commanded him: and **the Lord shut him in**."*
(Genesis 7:16)

We have here another aspect of *agapé*. Just as the Lord God closed the door and shut Noah and the cargo in, we see that He has shut us safely in too. It is He who does the sealing. No water will breach the Ark and nothing will come in as importantly as nothing will fall out. God designed the Ark to an exact specification. He knew in advance the pressures which the Ark would have to withstand and He knows the pressures which we will have to withstand in the seas of this present life. *Agapé* has budgeted for the tempests and you can be assured that *agapé* bears all things.

Q: What difference would it make to your life if you believe that God has already covered you for every eventuality which the storms and floods of life will throw up at you and that when the enemy comes in like a flood, He will raise a standard against it?

CHAPTER 24

AGAPÉ
ALWAYS BELIEVES
ALL THINGS

The implication of the truth of *agapé* is "breathtaking".

As the Apostle Paul continues to unveil the mystery of God's unconditional love, which He has for all He created, we are just left staggering under the weight of His love. Consider the statement before us. Not only does *agapé* bear all things, the Apostle Paul now reaches a new crescendo of absurdity by insisting that *agapé* believes all things. "What," you may ask, "does that mean?"

First, let me tell you straightaway what it does not mean. It does not mean that *agapé* is gullible or that we can pull the wool over its eyes. On the contrary, the absurdity of *agapé* is found in the realization that the One who knows us the best, loves us the most. What the Apostle Paul is saying here all but beggars belief, because the word "believe" literally means "to credit, to have confidence or to entrust oneself to another". *Agapé*, says the Apostle Paul, is impelled by a higher prerogative to entrust itself to us. Can you imagine that?! It is one thing for us to entrust ourselves to God, but surely it is mesmeric that God entrusts Himself to us?

Q: How do you feel knowing that even when you do not believe in God and nobody (including yourself) believes in you, God still does?

CHAPTER 25

AGAPÉ
ALWAYS HOPES

This deep-dive into the nature of God ought to leave us breathless. As we have already seen from the fathomless nature of God's loving nature, we are indeed safe and sound. We are close now to the summit and the thought that the Apostle Paul now introduces is quite extraordinary: "*Agapé*", he says, "always hopes." This must follow since it also believes all things and bears all things.

In modern usage, hope is a general feeling that some desire will be fulfilled. Without wishing to open a can of theological worms, I would say that God desires all men and women to come to the saving knowledge of His Son Jesus (1 Timothy 2:4). *Agapé* waits; always hoping and always knowing. Hope in this context means to wait for salvation with joy and full confidence. No wonder Abraham is called the friend of God (Isaiah 41:8) because as the Apostle Paul tells us:

"In hope [Abraham] believed against hope, that he should become the father of many nations, as he had been told, 'So shall your offspring be.' He did not weaken in faith when he considered his own body, which was as

147

*good as dead (since he was about a hundred years old),
or when he considered the barrenness of Sarah's womb.
No distrust made him waver concerning the promise of
God, but he grew strong in his faith as he gave glory to
God, fully convinced that God was able to do what He
had promised."*

(Romans 4:18-21)

When Abraham began his walk with God, his name was not
Abraham but Abram (Nehemiah 9:7). In changing his name,
God provided Abraham with a covenant sign and we may
also say, if you will permit the poetic license, that the inser-
tion of the *AH* into his name could stand as a reminder to us
that Abram and his wife, Sarai, had undergone a radical trans-
formation. They had, as it were, come to an understanding of
the mystery of the gospel that the apostle Paul would unveil:
the recognition of the indwelling life of Christ. Abraham, the
man of faith, was transformed from being an outer person, a
see-at-er (a person ruled by appearances) to becoming an inner
person, a *see-through*-er (a person who could see the invisible
and thus, believe for the impossible). He and Sarai saw that
Christ was their life. Through their crisis of circumstances they
came through to an inner-consciousness of Christ as their indwelling life and that recognition settled them in their faith and
in God's faithfulness. They had, what I would call, an "*ah,* I
see!" moment and so, Abram's name was changed to Abr-*ah!*-
am and Sarai to Sar*ah*! Pursuant of this thought Abraham comes
at last to the covenant sign of circumcision, to some a hallmark
of Israel's importance but to Abraham surely a sign and a daily
reminder of his impotence.

God the Father, the One who knows the end from the beginning, is the ultimate see-through-er and this should be a source of
great comfort and consolation to us to know that God Himself, by
nature, always hopes.

As Billy Graham once said, "I've read the last page of the Bible. It's all going to turn out all right."

Q: Are you encouraged to know that God knows He is not waiting in vain over you? How different would your life be if you begin to see yourself from God's perspective instead of from your own?

CHAPTER 26

AGAPÉ
ALWAYS ENDURES
ALL THINGS

Is there anything which love will not endure? No! *Agapé* endures all things as nothing can separate the loved one from the Lover. In saying that *agapé* endures all things, the Apostle Paul wants us to understand that the very words of Jesus – *"I will never leave you nor forsake you"* – is an axiom of *agapé*. He loves us, will remain with us and will abide in us. It is one of the great tragedies of contemporary Christianity that the message which has rung out is one of self-improvement. It is more of a brand; more *me*-ology than theology. An over-emphasis in some quarters on "me and what I can do" and the exultation of the triune anti-Christ of "me, myself and I" has given birth to our interpreting Scripture as a book on "How We Ought To Live" and on how Mankind can become good news to God when the appeal of the Bible from cover to cover is why God is Good News for Mankind. This characteristic of *agapé* provides us with a perfect example of our self-improving hermeneutics.

"Endurance" means "to persevere under misfortunes and trials". Is it not the case that when we think of endurance, we assume that it pertains to our holding fast to Christ through times of trials? But in truth, it pertains to the Father holding fast to His faith in Christ in us. When we know who we really are, *agapé* is enabled to endure and to bear bravely and calmly all our ill treatments of Him.

At this juncture I will raise a controversial issue. What, I wonder, are we to make of the inclusive nature of *agapé*? The Apostle Paul explicitly says that this endurance extends to all things. I appreciate that there are different interpretations of what "all things" actually means, but one cannot deny the universal aspect of *agapé*. Whether you conclude that "all things" refers to "all of a certain type" or to "each, every, any, all, the whole, everyone, all things and everything" is a debate for another day. What we can count on here, at the child level, is that you are home free.

Q: How does it feel knowing that you are home free?

CHAPTER 27

AGAPÉ
NEVER FAILS

Even for the most untrusting of pilgrims it is hard to imagine what further assurances would be required in order for them to finally enter into the rest of God, and thus, discover the *rest of God*. Surely the Apostle Paul has already furnished us with enough proof of God's love to silence the most doubting of all our Thomases but, as if in one grand finale, the Apostle Paul, standing on the very summit of Mount *Agapé*, sees one more view, one more vista, which simply staggers him. Seeing through the single eye of faith he says, "*Agapé* never fails." It is this statement which guarantees our victory and is the assurance that we will triumph.

The Apostle Paul declares from the mountain top, "God's divine grace never fails. For any reason whatsoever, His divine grace …

… can never ever fall to the ground powerless

… can never end

… is perpetual

… is eternal

153

… is always active

… is undiminished

… is unconditional

… is fixed

… can never be separated from you.

Q: For you, what does it mean to know that regardless of your failures, God's love will never fail concerning you?

This is the truth which the Child understands. Like Jacob resting on his staff and surveying the sheer wonder of God, we too must pause and survey the scene before us. We are now standing on the summit of this most remarkable mountain. I do not know of a more breathtaking vantage point anywhere else. Now, having made our way to the summit, I am reminded of my recent trip up to The Empire State Building's observatory in New York City. It took about ninety minutes of queuing to get to the elevator and as I queued up, there was this relentless petitioning to everyone there to buy an add-on guide under the dubious name of "Tony's, The Cabbie's Audio View" for an additional US$6.00. The pitch was "Know what you're looking at!" and it went on to say, "The view upstairs is great, but unless you know what you're looking at, it doesn't mean half as much!"

I decided to pay the extra US$6.00! I mean, what would be the point of standing on top of the world and having no idea what I was looking at? It proved to be the best US$6.00 I had ever spent. What an amazing audio tour! I learnt more about Manhattan Island in an hour than I would have learnt in a month. As I processed from vantage point to vantage point, I could not help but think of where we, at the Grace Project, were in our study of 1 Corinthians 13 and how, in the same way, *"the view upstairs is great but unless you know what you're looking at, it doesn't mean half as much!"* As with "Tony's, The Cabbie's Audio View" tour, so now, with us.

Back at the observatory, I was treated to a panoramic tour of the New York skyline – North to the Hudson River which flowed beneath the George Washington Bridge into New Jersey; East to the Borough of Queens and the beaches of Long Island; South-East to Brooklyn; West to Madison Square Garden; South to Wall Street, Ground Zero and the Statue of Liberty, Ellis Island; and so on. That hour brought Manhattan to life when the places of which I had heard and seen images all my life were before me and furthermore, contextualized.

Returning to our theme of *agapé*, here, at the top in *Agapé*'s observatory, let us look first to the foot of the mountain and what do we see? God's love for us, all of us, is unfailing because it endures forever and because God has entrusted Himself to us. He has committed Himself to us and will never renege on that promise. Consequently, delighted with His choice (which He has the luxury of making with the benefit of omniscience), He rejoices in all our circumstances, knowing that all things are working together for our good. He only thinks good of us and has no record of wrongs since *agapé* is unprovokable. *Agapé* (which is God being others-centred) is complete and is not rude. As a fixed other-lover, *agapé* is not proud, but rather, is happy to be vulnerable. In ways we simply cannot understand He, who needs nothing, has chosen to need us. *Agapé* is jealous for us and not of us. *Agapé* boasts about the apple of His eye to whom He is ever kind and, knowing all things, is eternally patient.

Thus, this is the first thing a Child knows. The Child knows the Father and by knowing the Father, the Child knows that He is love and the Child is loved. It is a tragedy for any Child to not know the love of his father. How much more tragic is it not to know the love of God. When this love comes into view, we will truly live at a higher level because perfect love casts out fear and one who fears cannot be perfected in love since fear has to do with punishment. As such, the Child proceeds to the next phase of life, knowing for certain that there is no condemnation.

Some years ago, my wife, Hayley, and I first visited Rio de Janeiro, Brazil and during that visit we went, as all tourists do, to see the Christo. Whilst at the site of the 320-foot statue of Christ the Redeemer, we were awed. It was impressive. What really captured my imagination was the ride in the cable car to the top of the mountain. On entering the cable car the guide told us that we would come to a point in the journey called the "Cor!" and when we arrived at that point, it would simply take our breath away. Being the cynic that I was, I prepared myself for what I was sure to be an anti-climax. Slowly but purposefully, the little cable car dragged itself up the mountain, making its way through the undergrowth. As it continued to journey further and further into the greeneries, everyone in the cable car had a sense that something spectacular was about to come into view. Little monkeys played in the foliage. Water coursed down the rocks. Suddenly and unexpectedly, the cable car broke through the undergrowth and burst out into the open. Everybody in the cable car snatched their breath and whooped an exclamation equivalent to "Cor!" Before us, the landscape of Rio de Janeiro did indeed take our breath away. Several minutes later, as we were still trying to take in all the sights before us, we reached the summit and there we stood at the feet of the statue of Christ.

How apt a metaphor this is for the Child who realizes that the Father loves him because He is love and the Child now stands at the feet of Christ, having been readied for the revelation of the characteristic of the next phase of spiritual maturity. What exhilaration awaits the Child as he realizes that since *agapé* never ends, never fails, never falls to the ground powerless, is eternal, constant, perpetual, everlasting, not temporal, is other worldly, always active, undiminished, unconditional and God is love, the Child can never act unlovingly to anyone, ever! In such a paradigm, the Child is bound to conclude that the concepts of unending love and unending punishment are incompatible. The Child is free from torment and knows, in the words of Solomon, that many waters cannot quench God's love and neither can floods drown it. What a revelation the Child has happened upon! In contrast to his contemporaries in the religious system, he has discovered that when Jesus spoke of the Parable of the Merchant (Matthew 13:46), He did not intend for His listeners to think that they must follow the example of the merchant and sell all they have so as to gain the pearl of great price which is salvation. It is sufficient for the Child at this stage to understand that God the Father is the Merchant and the Child is the pearl of great price for whom God would and has willingly paid the ultimate price (the life of His Son) so as to secure the Child for Himself. The Child is His pearl of great price and His beloved treasure.

So, there we have it. The Child is safe and sound, secure in the knowledge that his sins have been forgiven by his loving Father. However, and this is a question that troubles many Christians, is the Child-believer eternally secure? Does he have what Bill Gillham famously calls "A Lifetime Guarantee"? Or, as with retail purchases, does the Child-believer need to take out some extra insurance to extend the warranty period? Let us answer this most pressing of questions as we attempt to resolve the Child Phase of our journey together.

CHAPTER 28

HAPPILY EVER AFTER

Stories which begin with "Once upon a time" normally finish with "happily ever after". Mine is no exception. As with all believers, my experience is that even as we journey through our individual Valleys of Baca (Psalm 84), God makes that place a spring.

My "Once upon a time" began in the midst of my desolation. It is a rags-to-*true*-riches story. It is a story where hope replaces fear; where I am secure in the knowledge that I am safe and sound. That, dear reader, is a precious feeling because I have spent so much of my childhood being afraid.

Some time ago, I had the opportunity to meet the chairman of a major financial institution to speak with him about his company's emotional culture. I asked him what culture he wanted to create. I was riveted by his answer. He said, "I want this to be a place where nobody is afraid." Something resonated inside of me. Then, I asked him, "On a scale of one to ten, where is your company now?"

"Two," he replied ruefully.

He was right. I had worked with many of his top executives.

In contrast to the executives living in a world where they are taught to not trust in the living God but in uncertain riches (1 Timothy 6:17), spiritual children are *"storing up treasure for themselves as a good foundation for the future, so that they may take hold of that which is truly life"* (1 Timothy 6:19).

159

For now, suffice it for them to luxuriate in the exquisite truth that ...

"There is therefore now no condemnation for those who are in Christ Jesus. For the law of the Spirit of life has set you free in Christ Jesus from the Law of sin and death. For God has done what the Law, weakened by the flesh, could not do. By sending His own Son in the likeness of sinful flesh and for sin, He condemned sin in the flesh, in order that the righteous requirement of the Law might be fulfilled in us, who walk not according to the flesh but according to the Spirit. For those who live according to the flesh set their minds on the things of the flesh, but those who live according to the Spirit set their minds on the things of the Spirit. For to set the mind on the flesh is death, but to set the mind on the Spirit is life and peace."

(Romans 8:1-6)

"Christianity is not a religion; it's the proclamation of the end of religion. Religion is a human activity dedicated to the job of reconciling God to humanity and humanity to itself. The Gospel, however – the Good News of our Lord and Saviour Jesus Christ – is the astonishing announcement that God has done the whole work of reconciliation without a scrap of human assistance. It is the bizarre proclamation that religion is over, period."[5]

It is an irony of perverse proportions that the devil has managed to convince unbelievers that they are "secure" concerning salvation while, at the same time, persuading believers that their salvation is by no means secure and that whilst it may have been granted by grace, it could be withdrawn due to dis-grace. The satanic argument runs something like this –

5   Robert Farrar Capon, The Astonished Heart, (William B. Eerdmans Publishing Company, Grand Rapids, Michigan; 1996), p.2.

The devil to the unbeliever:

"I appreciate that you might not act like a saint on the outside but, deep down inside, you're a good person. Admittedly, you're not a churchgoer or anything like that but let's face it, this God whom the Christians go on about is reckoned to be the God of Love. So, *you might not be good enough to go to heaven but surely you're not bad enough to go to hell.* You're a good person deep down and that must count for something."

The devil to the believer:

"I appreciate that you might be trying to act like a saint on the outside but you and I both know that your mind is a sewer. Admittedly, you are a churchgoer but let's face it, though this God of yours might be the God of Love, He's not an idiot! Everybody knows that the road to hell is paved with good intentions. So, *you might not be bad enough to go to hell but how can you be sure you're good enough to go to heaven?* I'd watch my step if I were you. How can you be sure that enough's enough to get you into heaven?"

It really is ingenious. The unsaved world lives with a false sense of security while the saved community lives with a false sense of insecurity. The latter then seeks to evangelize the former and wonders why its attempts are met with such derision. The plain truth is that the true Church is a collective noun for those who have recognized the universal truth that God has done in Christ for Man what Man in his religion could not do for himself, *viz.* reconcile himself to God.

The tragedy of the Christian religion, in common with all the world religions, is its assertion that its rites, rituals and sacrifices have efficacy in and of themselves. It is for that reason alone

I find myself increasingly disassociating myself with the term "Christianity". In our contemporary setting, this term seems to be an increasingly misleading signature.

I have been campaigning for and will continue to press on for *"Christ without Christianity"* and this petition is all the more urgent in these days when what is generally being promoted under the banner of "Christianity" is, in fact, *"Christianity without Christ"*.

The title of this book, *Safe and Sound*, has been carefully chosen because unless we know we are safe, we cannot be sound. In this book, I suggest that in the "Little Children" phase, the happy effect of knowing the Father and knowing that our sins have been forgiven is that we have discovered, in the words of the Apostle Paul, "the riches of full assurance" (Colossians 2:2) where we are anchored in the reality of "no condemnation". The Child knows for certain that *"... since we have been justified by faith, we have peace with God through our Lord Jesus Christ. Through Him we have also obtained access by faith into this grace in which we stand, and we rejoice in hope of the glory of God"* (Romans 5:1-2). Consequently, the Child is "Eternally Secure".

The Child has received the first instalment of his inheritance, *viz.* Assurance – a life free from fear. As he matures, he will have access to yet greater treasures:

"Him we proclaim, warning everyone and teaching everyone with all wisdom, that we may present everyone mature in Christ. For this I [Paul] toil, struggling with all His energy that He powerfully works within me. For I want you to know how great a struggle I have for you and for those at Laodicea and for all who have not seen me face to face, that their hearts may be encouraged, being knit together in love, to reach all the riches ...."

(Colossians 1:28-2:2a)

What are these riches which the Apostle Paul sees us reaching for?

◊ The riches of full assurance (Colossians 2:2b);

◊ The riches of understanding (Colossians 2:2b); and

◊ The riches of the knowledge of God's mystery, which is Christ, in whom are hidden all the treasures of wisdom and knowledge (Colossians 2:3).

Having grasped the concepts contained and explained in this book which you, dear reader, may have gleaned from here or elsewhere, you have completed what I refer to as the Child Phase. You would have moved from the *calculating what's-in-it-for-me* self to the *real* or *true what's-in-me-for-you* self. You have therefore reached a state of full assurance – confidence. You are ready to progress to the next phase which is Understanding, which is Competence, the Teenager's Revelation.

◊ The Child's Revelation: Confidence – Full Assurance
   (Until Christ Is Formed: Part 1)

◊ The Teenager's Revelation: Competence – Understanding
   (Until Christ Is Formed: Part 2)

◊ The Father's Revelation: Confidants – Knowledge of the Mystery of God
   (Until Christ Is Formed: Part 3)

Until believers are settled in the question of their eternal security (i.e. that they are "safe"), they cannot be said to be "sound". It is impossible for believers to grow in grace as long as they harbour any anxiety or uncertainty about their position in Christ. Until you are sure of your salvation, you cannot grow in grace. Moreover, as long as one is fearful, one cannot be perfected in love. There is no fear in love for perfect love casts out fear and fear has to do with punishment (1 John 4:18). Note that the first and most tangible benefit believers receive is that they have "peace with God" (Romans 5:1).

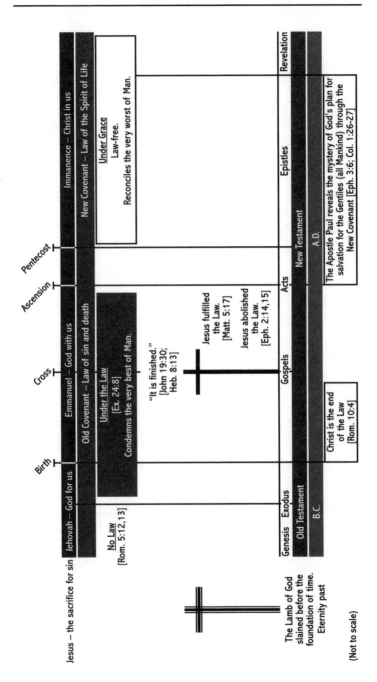

CHAPTER 29

WHO IS RESPONSIBLE FOR OUR SALVATION?

The one crucial diagnostic question telling us if we are ready to graduate from the "Little Children" phase is this: "Who is responsible for our salvation?" Our response to this question will reveal a great deal because it will reveal to us who or in what we are trusting for our salvation. I would like to emphasize that when I speak of salvation, I mean it in the 100% sense: "I am saved, I am being saved and I will be saved." In the book of Isaiah, the Lord set out the counter-intuitive way of grace and the Prophet Isaiah gave us Natural Man's response.

> *"For thus said the Lord God, the Holy One of Israel, 'In* **returning** *and* **rest** *you shall be saved; in* **quietness** *and in* **trust** *shall be your strength.' But you were unwilling, and you said, 'No! ....'"*

(Isaiah 30:15)

Israel's rebelliousness had made her choose not to hear the Lord's instruction and, much like today, tell her seers not to see, and had instructed her prophets to not prophesy what was right. With Israel turning aside from the path while trusting in herself, the Prophet Isaiah prescriptively set out the restorative way of grace.

> *"In **returning** [in retirement or withdrawal from our works] and [in] **rest** [in perfect stillness, even a death] shall you be saved ...."*
>
> (Isaiah 30:15a)

It is the Sabbath rest which David urges us to strive to enter into and that can only be experienced by pilgrims who have rested from their works as God did from His (Hebrews 4:7-10). The Prophet Isaiah said that this salvation, this liberation and deliverance, was accomplished by a retirement from works and a dying to self-effort. It is in *quietness* (meaning "in tranquillity, utterly undisturbed") and in *trust* that we shall find our might and our valour to execute the mighty deeds of God. Yet, in an act of eccentric defiance, Israel's emphatic response was, "No, that is not how we will live the spiritual life! We will not retire, will not rest, will not be quiet and will not place our confidence in God." Instead, Israel proposed an alternative strategy, i.e., rather than dressing herself in the riches of grace, she chose to outfit herself in the rags of religion.

Israel: "We will flee upon horses."
Consequence: "Therefore, you shall flee away!"

Israel: "We will ride upon swift steeds."
Consequence: "Therefore, your pursuers shall be swift!"

> *"A thousand shall flee at the threat of one; at the threat of five you shall flee, till you are left like a flagstaff on the top of a mountain, like a signal on a hill."*
>
> (Isaiah 30:17)

In the Prophet Isaiah's allusion, Israel's obstinacy had left her desolate like a flagstaff on the top of a mountain, defeated and deflated, and herein lies the great lesson of the way of grace. Not only did the Lord oversee Israel's defeat, He watched and waited patiently for her so as to show her mercy. The Prophet Isaiah tells us,

> *"Therefore the Lord waits to be gracious to you, and therefore He exalts Himself to show mercy to you. For the Lord is a God of justice [good judgement and full of grace]; blessed are all those who wait for Him"*
>
> (Isaiah 30:18)

Of all the grace lessons I have ever had to come to terms with, this is certainly among the most difficult. I was so wedded to self-effort and self-authentication that it was necessary for Him to allow me to be swallowed up with the pain of trying to make my life work apart from Him before I would turn to Him.

As a parent, I accept that there are moments in the raising of children which call for harsh discipline. Incidentally, do not think that a life of grace means that we are exempt from discipline. On the contrary. Just as Law and punishment go together, so are grace and discipline synonymous. Moreover, although punishment and discipline, when administered, may both feel the same, they are not. The Law is punitive whilst all actions of grace are restorative. In any event, this discipline is often more painful to administer than to receive and I suspect that there have been many times over the years when it has grieved the heart of God to have to discipline me but the gain (i.e., obedience to faith) is worth the pain. The blunt and frank truth is that the principal drivers of change are pain and remedy. The reason why people change what they do is due less to their being given analysis which shifts their thinking but rather that they are shown a truth which influences their feelings.

> **"People change when they hurt enough to be willing to, when they learn enough to want to and when they are affirmed enough to be empowered to."**

So says the Prophet Isaiah, *"Blessed are all those who wait for Him."* It is an axiom which the prophet will reiterate in his vivid imagery in chapter 40. There, he depicts the youths fainting and growing weary from self-effort and the young men falling exhausted; all in contrast to those who wait upon the Lord exchanging their strength for God's and in so doing, *"mount up with wings like eagles; they shall run and not be weary; they shall walk and not faint."* This prospect is open to all who will simply allow themselves to be mastered by the way of grace and cease from their labours. The only desire of the Lord is to bless us, but He blesses on His own terms and herein lies the conundrum – what He calls a blessing, we often think of being accursed and *vice versa.* Typically, we will go to Him with our *wants* and invariably, He will meet our *needs.* At first, this is perplexing because often what we want is not what we need and what we need is not what we want. Be that as it may, as we grow spiritually, our needs and our wants are integrated. Thus, there must be an aligning of hearts and minds – ours with His – and this alignment invariably involves encouraging us to stop relying on ourselves (2 Corinthians 1:8-10), a goal which He is ruthless in His pursuit of.

However, the divine consolation is that ...

> *"For a people shall dwell in Zion, in Jerusalem; you shall weep no more. He will surely be gracious to you at the sound of your cry. As soon as He hears it, He answers you."*
>
> (Isaiah 30:19)

Is this not the anguished lament of the Apostle Paul, *"Wretched man that I am! Who will deliver me ...?"* (Romans 7:24). Surely it is. Then, at that moment,

"Though the Lord gives you the bread of adversity and the water of affliction, yet your Teacher will not hide Himself anymore, but your eyes shall see your Teacher. And your ears shall hear a word behind you, saying, 'This is the way, walk in it,' when you turn to the right or when you turn to the left. Then you will defile your carved idols overlaid with silver and your gold-plated metal images. You will scatter them as unclean things. You will say to them, 'Be gone!'"

(Isaiah 30:20-22)

However, to reach that point, we must end our fatal love affair with self-effort. So, here is a question for you to ponder – is salvation a work of God for Man, a work of Man for God or a joint-venture between both parties?

Salvation is the work of ...

... God, not me – all of God and none of me.

... Me, not God – all of me and none of God.

... God and Me – some of God and some of me.

There is a great deal at stake in our answer. I am firmly of the view that the character of God (i.e., *agapé*) and the nature of salvation (*viz.* a free gift of grace [Eph. 2:8]) insist that salvation is an absurd, extravagant, display of God's love, is all of God and none of Man and once given, this gift cannot be rescinded.

CHAPTER 30

CAST IRON ASSURANCE

Once, whilst teaching on this subject, I was interrupted by a student in the middle of my talk. Incandescent with indignation, he blurted out, "Enough is enough!" I was a little startled. When I questioned him as to why he objected he said words to the effect that "I know what you're leading us to. You're going to tell us that we cannot lose our salvation and that is just too much to put up with. People must speak out against this kind of teaching."

"Oh," I said. "Sorry, but I didn't mean to upset you by telling you that God loves you." Mollified, my young friend was not; anything but! In the end, it transpired that he, like many Christians, was of the view that to teach the truth that "the believer is eternally secure" is to preach a license to sin.

Quite apart from my not being sympathetic to the assumed correlation between freedom from the Law and freedom to sin, the real issue regarding salvation is not the character and quality of an individual's behaviour but the *character of God* and the *quality of the salvation He gives*. In order for God's love to be unconditional, it must, by definition, be independent of anything we do or do not do. Therefore, to doubt the security of one's salvation is to doubt the character of God and call Him a liar (see John 3:15; John 10:28; Titus 1:2; 1 John 5:11-13).

> Q: Did you respond to the call of a god who rewards the righteous or the God who justifies the wicked?

> Q: If my unfaithfulness has a bearing on my salvation (and therefore, my relationship with God), is it correct to call His love for me "unconditional"?

> "If (God's) holiness demands something in return from those He loves, it is clear that His holiness makes God incapable of unconditional love! If holiness is a condition, His love is not unconditional. If His nature forces Him to disassociate with certain types of people, His nature stands in the way of His ability to love unconditionally."[6]

Safe and Sound in the Love of God (Romans 8:35-39)

"Who shall separate us from the love of Christ? Shall tribulation, or distress, or persecution, or famine, or nakedness, or danger, or sword? As it is written, 'For your sake we are being killed all the day long; we are regarded as sheep to be slaughtered.' No, in all these things we are more than conquerors through Him who loved us. For I am sure that neither death nor life, nor angels nor rulers, nor things present nor things to come, nor powers, nor height nor depth, nor anything else in all creation, will be able to separate us from the love of God in Christ Jesus our Lord."

6   Charles Stanley, Eternal Security – Can You Be Sure? (Large Print Edition), (Walker & Company, New York; 1999), pp. 16-17.

There cannot be a more emphatic declaration of assurance in the entire Bible than the one above, for in these few verses, the Apostle Paul concretizes our position in Christ. Just for the moment, let us follow his rhetorical question and answer session.

Q: Who will separate us from the love of Christ?

A: Nobody!

Q: What will separate us from the love of God?

A: Nothing!

Q: What are the circumstances which can separate us? Can hardship, distress, persecution, famine, nakedness, peril or sword separate us from the love of God?

A: Absolutely not!

If hardship, distress, persecution, famine, nakedness, peril and sword could not separate the apostles from loving the Church with the love of God and if it did not separate the faithful remnant (who, in adversity and oppression, became convinced of the futility of self-effort – Psalm 44) from loving God (Psalm 44:22), how could the same pressures ever separate Christ, who is love, from loving us? Indeed, is it not precisely because He loves us that He has gladly suffered all these things for us? God is for us and if God is for us, who can be against us? Even our own self-destructive strategies cannot thwart His love purposes for us. Having endured so much for the joy (i.e., us) set before him, why would He then separate Himself from us?

The Apostle Paul is not talking about whether we will stop loving God and thus, run the risk of God stopping His love for us. He is saying that God will never stop loving us even if we stop loving Him. God is faithful even to the faithless.

CHAPTER 31

GROWING GRACEFULLY

We must keep in view that salvation is the free gift of God and the nature of that gift is *His life*. Moreover, this gift is not a loan repayable on easy terms nor given to us on a trial basis. It is a gift given freely and without reservation. This gift, which is His life, is given to us not that we might imitate it but that we might *participate* in it (2 Peter 1:4).

Growth in this life depends on, what I call, an ever-expanding awareness of who we already are. Simply put, spiritual growth is growing in grace (2 Peter 3:18). However, how much we grow in grace is inexorably linked to how much we know ourselves to be safe and sound in respect of our salvation.

A believer must, first, be settled in the elementary principles of faith. To this end, some simple diagnostic questions may be asked:

	Always	Often	Occasionally	Never
To what extent do I experience peace with God?				
To what extent has perfect love cast out fear in my life?				
To what extent do I believe that salvation is wholly a work of God for Mankind?				

(Perhaps you are not pleased by your answers, but that may be because the idea of being free in Christ is still new to you. Maybe you have more sympathy with Joyce Meyer's comment that "There was a time when I never felt right unless I felt wrong.")

> *"But when Christ appeared as a High Priest of the good things that have come, then through the greater and perfect tent (not made with hands, that is, not of this creation) He entered **once for all** into the holy place, not by means of the blood of goats and calves but by means of His own blood, thus securing an **eternal redemption.**"*
>
> (Hebrews 9:11-12)

Eternal – perpetual, unending, everlasting, undying, unceasing
Redemption – to be released from an obligation

Unlike His Levitical counterparts who sacrificed the blood of bulls and goats in a tabernacle (which was a copy of heavenly things), our High Priest offered Himself up as the perfect sacrifice. He did this *once for all* and obtained eternal release for all humanity from their obligation to sin.

The quality of salvation depends on the quality of the Saviour, not the sinner.

Because Jesus Christ has obtained redemption for us, our faith and hope are not based on ourselves or any other human being but our faith and hope are in God (1 Peter 1:21). Furthermore, we can be safe and sound because we know that our salvation was not purchased with anything temporal ... *"[we] were ransomed ... not with perishable things such as silver or gold"* (1 Peter 1:18) but rather, with the blood of Jesus.

CHAPTER 32

WHAT DO I
HAVE TO DO?

The great satanic deception is to get the Christian to serve God
so as to earn what cannot, or indeed, need not, be earned since
Christ has already earned it on our behalf. 2 Peter 1:3 clearly
states that we have already received everything which God has
for us pertaining to our salvation. We cannot work to receive
more because He has given all and He will not remove what He
has already given.

Holiness – An Obstacle to Eternal Security

Many who oppose the teaching of "Justification by Faith"
would insist that such a "holy action" (salvation) demands an
equal "holy reaction" (holy living). The belief is that although
salvation is obtained by faith, it is to be confirmed and main-
tained by "holy living" (i.e. works) thus making holiness a
condition for maintaining salvation. The unfortunate implication of this is that if the Christian's relationship with God is
dependent upon the holiness of the Christian, God's love is,
therefore, not unconditional.

Given the great proliferation of "holiness" teaching in the
Church today, it might come as a surprise to note that the word

"holy" appears only eight times in the New Testament. More importantly, when mentioned in the Bible, the word "holiness" is never accompanied by a threat.

Kittles Dictionary of the New Testament:

> *"Holiness is not something we must strive to either attain or maintain in the same way in which we, as Christians, do not get forgiven. We are forgiven. We do not become holy. We are holy!"*

The clarion call for holy living is, no doubt, sincere but it is, sadly, a stumbling block to living. There is no New Testament warrant for "holiness" teaching. The determination for "self-to-live-a-holy-life" will invariably cause confusion and bewilderment which, counter-intuitively, are their only true value.

Motivation for Holy Living – Fear

A common belief by much of the Church is that what will motivate believers to live a "holy" life is the *fear of losing* their salvation. It may have been argued (or at least, insinuated) that a little fear is healthy, but fear has to do with punishment and a person who fears cannot be perfected in love (1 John 4:18). As the Apostle Paul discovered, even if one can become a perfect Law-keeper, it is of no value (Philippians 3:4-8).

There are many spiritual ministers and teachers who, although privately believing the Doctrine of Eternal Security, do not teach it for fear that Christians will live unholy lives and that a Law-free gospel equates a lawless living.

Yet, this is surely a simple dilemma to resolve. If somebody is presented with the truth and their response is to behave irresponsibly, that must, of necessity, point to the immaturity of the hearer rather than the truth of the message. To withhold truth is a greater crime than to abuse it. There will always be those who view grace as anti-holiness and as giving the licence to sin. Some might even call it a "Sinner's Charter". The Apostle Peter responded to these false teachers in 2 Peter 3:15-16.

> *"And count the patience of our Lord as salvation, just as our beloved brother Paul also wrote to you according to the wisdom given to him, as he does in all his letters when he speaks in them of these matters. There are some things in them that are hard to understand, which the ignorant and unstable twist to their own destruction, as they do the other Scriptures."*

We must not confuse righteous works with "works of righteousness". Yet, sadly, it is the latter which is the very thing being promoted as an aide to bring us closer to God and which has precisely the opposite effect. Paradoxically, "holiness" teaching is actively, although unwittingly, campaigning against God's purpose of conforming believers into the image of Christ (Romans 8:29). Love and Fear do not mix any more than Grace and Law.

Does Grace Promote Sin?

The Apostle Paul responded to the question I stated above, in Romans 6:1-2:

> *"What shall we say then? Are we to continue in sin that grace may abound? By no means! How can we who died to sin still live in it?"*

Understanding the grace of God brings freedom and that freedom, rather than stirring up the flesh, empowers us to love and love thinks not of itself but instead, says, "It's not about me; it's about you." Love seeks to serve and bless others rather than take and offend (1 Corinthians 13:4-7).

Growing Gracefully – Questions

Q: Are Christians to imitate or to participate in the life of Christ? Is there a difference?

Q: To mature as a Christian, do I need to become more holy? Why?

Q: If we believe that we can lose our salvation, what is the only motivation for holy living?

But What About …?

A clamour of protest will always be heard from those who believe that the free gift of grace can be forfeited. They will refer to what I call the "But what about …?" verses – their particular favourite being Hebrews 6:4-6. It is a perverse malady and sad contortion of the religious mind that it seeks to find reasons to be anxious. This incessant need to do something to convince God of their self-worth causes them to hijack Scriptural passages and fly them into church buildings, destroying all in their wake.

I greatly suspect that Hebrews 6:4 has been commandeered in the same misguided way as Hebrews 7 has been recruited to teach tithing as a New Covenant principle[7] when Hebrews 7 has nothing to do with tithing any more than Hebrews 6:4-6 is a discussion on eternal security. Hebrews 7 is simply overlaying the argument of the writer to the Hebrews that Jesus' dispensation of grace and truth surpasses and outclasses the Mosaic dispensation of the Law (John 1:17).

Calvin understood that the purpose of Hebrews was not to convince the Jewish readers that Jesus Christ was the Promised Redeemer, but rather to show them what that meant, i.e., what exactly Jesus' death and resurrection did accomplish. It is evident

---

7   See Paul Anderson-Walsh, the Appendix to The Bonsai Conspiracy (Grapho, São Paolo, Brazil; 2006), p. 217.

that the Jewish readers did not understand and it seems equally clear that the letter to the Hebrews survives today as a means of fully evangelizing anybody who ...

... is still clinging to the Law as a means of procuring righteousness;

... is possessed of a lavish and inflated view of both the purpose and status of the Law (which can make nothing perfect but rather, to prove that nobody can make themselves perfect through it);

... has an impoverished view of the death and resurrection of Jesus (which has made perfect forever those who are being made holy – Hebrews 10:14);

... considers the Law to be operative still when actually it is obsolete as the way to and of righteousness (Hebrews 8:13);

... is living in the shadowlands of the Law and not the Promised Land of Grace;

... is struggling with the consciousness of sin;

... is burdened by the need to feel forgiven;

... is lacking assurance;

... does not always feel very saved because of his or her behaviour;

... is not experiencing the abundant life of Jesus Christ.

In short, Hebrews is a book written to and for those of us who have not realized the absolute finality of the cross without which there is no prospect of resting in the reality of the resurrection. It is for those of us who still need to recognize that the goal of the Christian life is simply to believe in the lasting efficacy of the sacrificial death and resurrection of our Lord Jesus Christ and enter into His Sabbath rest. The writer to the Hebrews is seeking to persuade us that we no longer need to live a religious life, but rather accept that Christ is our life and come boldly before the throne of grace and find help in time of need. The writer's purpose is to demonstrate that either the cross has said it all or has said nothing at all and by calling the covenant "New", the "Old" has become defunct and obsolete (Hebrews 8:13).

However, so insatiable is the religious appetite for the offal of Legalism that even if Satan cannot keep us from realizing that we are under the New Covenant, he has little difficulty in persuading us that we must try to live under both the Old and New Covenants simultaneously. In response, the writer to the Hebrews insists that we cannot live under both. We have to make up our minds – either we live under the Law or under grace but we cannot live under both for nobody can serve two masters.

Notwithstanding the fact that nowhere in the Scriptures do we find Law and grace mingled, the overwhelming majority of Christians live as though the Covenants have been conjugated instead of recognizing that the Law has been abrogated. Nowhere in the Scriptures will we see the two covenants conflated. To mix Law and grace is to both rob the Law of its terror and denude grace of its freedom. How can two such contrary concepts be harmonized?

Under the Law, we try to make ourselves acceptable to God only to discover that we cannot do so, whilst under grace we cannot but accept that God has made us acceptable. Grace is God giving righteousness whilst the Law is God demanding it. Right-standing is given by grace and not works. We either stand in His righteousness or in ours but we cannot stand in both.

It is for these reasons (and more) that the writer to the Hebrews affirms that Jesus is indeed superior in every way to the Old Covenant Levi because Jesus ...

... is the better Messenger with a better message

(Hebrews 1:1-2:18);

... is the better Apostle (Hebrews 3:1-4:13) as evidenced by His superiority to Moses;

... is the better Priest compared to Aaron and Melchizedek, better oath and better sacrifice (Hebrews 4:14-7:28);

... is the better Covenant (Hebrews 8:1-9:28, contrasting the New and Old Covenants);

... is the better Sacrifice (Hebrews 10:1-31, the potency of Christ contrasted with the impotency of the Law);

... is the better Way (Hebrews 10:32-12:29, essentially, faith versus works);

... provides a better way of life (Hebrews 13:1-25, faith object and action).

To prosecute his case, the writer to the Hebrews provides the court with no fewer than one hundred and forty-four Old Testament quotations and allusions whilst his opening arguments leave the court of religious opinion in little doubt as to what verdict to return. He presents irrefutable testimony that Jesus is a better messenger and the New Covenant has outclassed the Old Covenant in every regard. The writer to the Hebrews sets forth Jesus' provenance beyond all reasonable doubt, demonstrating that Jesus ...

... is the Son (Hebrews 1:2) and therefore, speaks with greater
authority than the prophets;

... is the Heir of all things (Hebrews 1:2);

... is the Creator of the universe and therefore God (John 1:3); the
Architect is greater than the building and He created Abraham,
Moses, Levi, the Temple and everything in it;

... is the exact imprint (carbon copy) of God's very being (Colossians 1:15; Philippians 2:6);

... is the sustainer of all things by His powerful word;

... is the Master of the universe;

... has made purification for sins (this is the first reference to His
soteriological purpose for coming; He has accomplished what
no prophet, priest, king or angel could, and by the one sacrifice,
He has made forever perfect all those who are being made holy
– Hebrews 10:14).

Turning to the sixth chapter as his argument gains momentum, the
writer to the Hebrews says,

*"Therefore let us leave the elementary doctrine of Christ and
go on to maturity, not laying again a foundation of repentance
from dead works and of faith towards God, and of instruction
about washings, the laying on of hands, the resurrection of
the dead, and eternal judgment. And this we will do, if God
permits. For it is impossible to restore again to repentance
those who have once been enlightened, who have tasted the
heavenly gift, and have shared in the Holy Spirit, and have
tasted the goodness of the word of God and the powers of the*

age to come, if they then fall away, since they are crucifying once again the Son of God to their own harm and holding Him up to contempt. For land that has drunk the rain that often falls on it, and produces a crop useful to those for whose sake it is cultivated, receives a blessing from God. But if it bears thorns and thistles, it is worthless and near to being cursed, and its end is to be burned. Though we speak in this way, yet in your case, beloved, we feel sure of better things – things that belong to salvation."

(Hebrews 6:1-9)

Now, let me ask a simple question: what was the writer's primary interest here? Surely it was not the issue of eternal security, but rather he was seeking to address the malignant thought which was spreading among the community that unless the Levitical sacrifices as prescribed in the Torah (the Law) were adhered to without deviation and to the letter, there would be no certainty that the people's sins would be forgiven. As we know, many of the epistles were written in response to questions and concerns which arose in the fledgling communities. This was the context into which the Apostle John wrote his first epistle. In my book entitled *The Bonsai Conspiracy*, I have dealt with the Apostle Paul's rebuttal of the agitators who had managed to infiltrate the Galatian community. Here, in the Hebrews setting, it seems that the people were also being coaxed back to being under the Law.

The entire tone of the epistle to the Hebrews betrays the communities' obsession with the need to make sacrifice for sin. The argument of Hebrews is that Jesus' *atonement* effected for all time the permanent *at-one-ment* with God and by Jesus having done so, the Levitical system is made redundant. In saying, "See, I have come to do Your will," Jesus *has abolished* the first in order to establish the second. The now obsolete Law is described as fading away for a good reason because although it is no longer legal tender, there is still a great deal of it in circulation. By analogy, when the Bank of England withdraws a note from circulation, they issue a date after which that note will no longer be accepted. Recently, the date for the withdrawal of the old £20 note was set for February 28th. Up until that time, one could spend the old £20 notes in the shops, but after that date they were no longer legal tender. From March 1st onwards, the old note has become invalid irretrievably. In the same way, we cannot bring the Levitical currency to the counter of heaven and expect it to be accepted.

The situation which confronted the Hebrew community is dire and requires some hard-talking. Allow me to offer my own paraphrase:

"Let me put this to you as crudely as I can and I make no apologies for doing so. This is a serious matter. I had envisaged that by now we would have dispensed with this kid's stuff and been pressing into the mature things of God. We should be on meat and not milk. I had hoped that our ministry to you would have been sufficient to enable you to leave behind the basic teaching about Christ and you would not be harping back to that old self-help rubbish which was, after all, only a ruse to get you to see sense and come to Christ. But here we are again. No wonder the Apostle Paul speaks about being in the pangs of childbirth. I feel like this business of being a Christ-planter is one long unending contraction pain without an epidural in sight.

Let me spell it out to you, my beloved. If what you are telling me is that even though having been enlightened, by which I mean, been given incontrovertible evidence that Jesus is the Messiah; and even though you have tasted the heavenly gift and knowing full well that the gift of God is eternal life; and even though you have shared in the Holy Spirit and have tasted the goodness of the word of God by biting into the sweet fruit of grace and seen that it was good; and even though you have seen the authentic manifestation of the Spirit so much so that you have even experienced the powers

WHAT DO I HAVE TO DO?   189

of the age to come, you think that on balance because of this itch you call the consciousness of sin that it would be best to return to the defunct never-did-anybody-any-good Levitical system, then you are out of your minds!

Even after having weighed up the evidence, you have resolved to reject the blood of Jesus in favour of the same tired old never-can-make-anything-perfect sacrifices of the blood of bulls and goats. And even though God Himself has told you in no uncertain terms that He has no interest in your meaningless self-improvement-God-mollification programmes and, in any case, He has done away with the whole rotten lot of it by the expedient offering of His own Son for us, you are, nonetheless, telling me that the Body of Christ you have no desire for but instead, the blood of bulls and goats have you prepared for Him. Well, if that really is your position, I have got to say, 'Houston, we have a problem' because you are holding Jesus in contempt, trampling on the Son of God and making His sacrificial death and resurrection a mockery and a laughing-stock. And brothers and sisters, let me tell you that as long as you insist on crucifying again and again the Son of God and holding Him up to contempt by trusting in this other stuff, it is impossible to renew you to repentance. So, knock yourself out!"

But What About Hebrews 6:4-6?
"Alright," I hear you say, "that was a fancy piece of avoiding-the-question footwork, but answer this question: Do these verses not prove that we can lose our salvation?"

No, they don't teach anything of the sort!

"Alright then, clever clogs, what do they mean?"

"For it is impossible to restore again to repentance those who have once been enlightened, who have tasted the heav-enly gift, and have shared in the Holy Spirit, and have tasted the goodness of the word of God and the powers of the age to come, if they then fall away, since they are crucifying

once again the Son of God to their own harm and holding
Him up to contempt."

(Hebrews 6:4-6)

Alright, try this on for size. At first glance, these verses appear to suggest that Christians could lose their salvation. However, to understand these verses, we need to consider the basis upon which we are saved. We are justified by faith apart from works, are we not? Justification means being made acceptable to a holy God, i.e., being made righteous (2 Corinthians 5:21). Moreover, we are saved by the Life of Christ (Romans 5:10). As such, I can say without fear of correction or contradiction that "to be saved" means "to be rescued completely from peril and returned to safety". Further, I can assert that the life which I now live is not my own life but Christ's Life (Galatians 2:20-21). Our understanding of this raises an important question: If what we do with our life cannot save us, how can what we do with it cause us to lose our salvation?

An example of this truth can be found in the Apostle Paul's writings to the church in Corinth where not only was one man openly sleeping with his step-mother, the man held it out as being illustrative of what it meant to be free in Christ and was venerated as a trophy of grace. One might say that Corinth was Law-*less* rather than Law-*free*. Nevertheless, when the Apostle Paul wrote his corrective letter to the Corinthians, he never took them back to Moses, i.e., he never put them under the Law and yet, he dealt with them firmly.

God affirms you before He afflicts you.

"I give thanks to my God always for you because of the grace
of God that was given you in Christ Jesus, that in every way
you were enriched in Him in all speech and all knowledge
– even as the testimony about Christ was confirmed among

you – so that you are not lacking in any spiritual gift [char-
ismata], as you wait for the revealing of our Lord Jesus, who
*will **sustain** [i.e., "validate", see also Philippians 1:6] you*
*to the end, **guiltless** in the day of our Lord Jesus Christ. God*
is faithful, by whom you were called into the fellowship of his
Son, Jesus Christ our Lord."

(1 Corinthians 1:4-9)

The Apostle Paul uses this passage to affirm and put the Corinthians safely into the matrix of Eternal Security by beginning his
appeal in the context of assurance before he rebukes and seeks to
correct them.

"Do you not know [the Apostle Paul uses this phrase nine
*times in Corinthians, but only once elsewhere] that **you***
*[plural] are God's **temple** [singular] ...."*

(1 Corinthians 3:16)

Although the believers in the church in Corinth are living lives
which are no doubt contrary to that expected of Christians, at no
time does the Apostle Paul make mention of the loss of salvation,
but rather he affirms them in their identity as children of God whilst
simultaneously rebuking them and trying to correct their error.

In view of this, I would suggest that Hebrews 6:4-6 does not
refer to the loss of salvation. This is all the more apparent when
we consider that if we were to take this text to mean that one
can lose one's salvation, we must also insist that it means "Once
lost, always lost"! Having "lost" our salvation, we could never
get it back as the Hebrews verses say that "it is impossible to
renew such one to repentance." Incidentally, is it not curious
that those who teach these as anti-security verses are also the
same folk who urge people to recommit their lives to Jesus after
having fallen away? What would be the point of that since no
one could be restored?

Let us look at the case of the Apostle Peter's denial (Matthew 26:69-75; Mark 14:66-72; Luke 22:55-62; John 18:15-18, 25-27). If no one could be restored after having "fallen away", we would have to do some serious rewriting of the New Testament because poor old Apostle Peter would be in some very hot water.

In Luke 22:31-33 how can we forget Jesus' pained voice when he said, *"Simon* [Peter]*, Simon* [Peter]*, behold, Satan demanded* [or obtained permission] *to have you, that he might sift you like wheat, but I have prayed for you that your faith may not fail. And when you have turned again, strengthen your brothers."* The Apostle Peter responded, *"Lord, I am ready to go with You both to prison and to death."* Yet, despite his bravado, the Apostle Peter proceeded to deny Jesus three times. The Apostle Peter had to learn two valuable lessons. He had to learn, 1. who he really was, and 2. that his faithlessness did not disqualify him. However, according to the "once lost, always lost" interpretation of Hebrews, the Apostle Peter would have fallen from grace and thus, by that reckoning, should have lost his salvation.

Moreover, these verses also say that it is impossible to "restore again to repentance" those who have fallen away. Therefore, if we were to accept that one can lose one's salvation, these verses must be saying, "Once saved, could be lost and if lost, always lost."

Therefore, to use these verses to argue that Christians can lose their salvation and then call the backslider to repentance is a contradiction of the verses, because according to the text itself, there is no second chance. To my mind at least, the fact that the verses also refer to those who have *"tasted the goodness of the word of God and the powers of the age to come"* does not necessarily mean that they are referring to a regenerate believer. Just like the ten spies who entered into the Promised Land (Deuteronomy 1:19-26), there are those who might have tasted the fruit but still do not believe. They are those who would come to the very threshold of faith only to turn back, experiencing the power of God in the flesh and yet, not coming to a spiritual faith encounter with Christ (Matthew 13:20-21). Consider the example of Judas (John 6:70-71; Acts 1:17) who plainly participated in the life and ministry of Jesus but was never saved.

A potential objection to my view here is that the writer to the Hebrews used the same word in chapter 2 verse 9 when speaking of Christ tasting death on our behalf. However, it is worth noting that although Jesus did die physically, He did not die spiritually and hence, likewise, it could be that a person might experience the power of God physically and yet, remain spiritually unregenerate.

However, I believe that my view is supported by the fact that the writer to the Hebrews began by saying, "Therefore let us leave the elementary doctrine of Christ and go on to maturity, not laying again a foundation of repentance from dead works and of faith towards God ..." (Hebrews 6:1).

If you do not understand the basis of your assurance in God you are in perilous danger. You have to understand that God does not look at our behaviour but, rather, He looks at our identity. Both the Apostle Peter and the church in Corinth are evidence of that.

*"For by grace you have been saved **through faith**. And this is not your own doing; it is the gift of God, not a result of works, so that no one may boast. For we are His workmanship, created in Christ Jesus for good works, which God prepared beforehand, that we should walk in them."*

(Ephesians 2:8-10)

"... by God's power [we] are being guarded through faith ...."

(1 Peter 1:5)

"... [Let us look] to Jesus, the Founder and Perfecter of our faith."

(Hebrews 12:2a)

Chapter 33

The Defence Rests

Earlier, I stated that mine is a story which ends with "happily ever after" and, dear reader, so does yours. In spite of where you may be at this precise moment, there is every reason to be cheerful rather than fearful. The fact that you are safe and sound rests on the following four immutable tenets:

The omniscience of God – God is *all knowing*.

The omnipotence of God – God is *all powerful*.

The individual Members of the Trinity all work together for your good.

The nature of God – God is *all loving* and *loving all*.

The Omniscience of God

Omniscience is a theological term referring to God's superior knowledge and wisdom which are His power to know all things, i.e., God is all knowing. Simply put, God knows everything there is to know about everything there is to know. God knows Himself and all things actual and possible in one simple and eternal act.

He is perfect in *knowledge* (Job 37:16).

He *knows* everything (1 John 3:20).

All this means that even before the foundation of time, God knew everything each individual would do throughout the course of his or her life (Psalm 139:16). He knew every event in world history and nothing existed outside of Him. However, the fact that He knows what I am going to do does not, in any way, compromise my freewill. He does not make my choices for me but He knows what choices I will make.

"O Lord, You have searched me and known me! You know when I sit down and when I rise up; You discern my thoughts from afar."

(Psalm 139:1-2)

In many ways, this makes God's gift of salvation all the more remarkable since God's decision to save us is based on facts, not feelings. He is not like disillusioned spouses who file for divorce because their partners turn out to be someone other than who they thought they were.

Regardless of what any of us would conclude about salvation, all will agree that God has designed it in the light of all the facts of Mankind. We need to remember that we serve a God who does not reward the self-righteous but justifies the wicked (Romans 4:5).

Fundamental to our understanding of salvation is our recognition that we are not sinners in need of a Saviour, but that He was and is a Saviour in need of sinners. This is something we tend to overlook. We must remember that Jesus was, in fact, slain before the foundation of time. The effect of this is obvious. Let us draw a contemporary illustration by using the outbreak of the S.A.R.S. (avian flu) virus as an example. Scientists everywhere are working extensively to find a cure. Until that cure is found, nobody is safe.

In the case of sin, the reverse is true – God had already prepared the vaccine even before there was a virus and thus, in the case of Redemption, we have, in fact, a vaccine in need of a disease.

God's omniscience ensures that He is "shock proof". He is never surprised by anything we do, good or bad, because He knows all things from the beginning to the end and yet He still chooses us. As my friend, Steve McVey, puts it, "Did it ever occur to you that nothing ever occurred to God?"

God is never caught unawares by our sin. His faithfulness is neither dependent on our faithfulness nor compromised by our unfaithfulness.

> *"If we are faithless, He remains faithful for He cannot deny Himself."*

> (2 Timothy 2:13)

The Omnipotence of God

Omnipotence is the term which refers to the all-encompassing power and sovereignty of God. His omnipotence is closely connected to His omniscience because not only is He all-knowing, He is also all-powerful (*cf.* Genesis 18:14; Jeremiah 32:17). The book of Isaiah speaks of these two characteristics of God.

> *"Remember the former things of old; for I am God, and there is no other; I am God, and there is none like Me, declaring the end from the beginning and from ancient times things not yet done, saying, 'My counsel shall stand, and I will accomplish all My purpose', calling a bird of prey from the east, the man of My counsel from a far country. I have spoken, and I will bring it to pass; I have purposed, and I will do it. Listen to Me, you stubborn of heart, you who are far from righteousness. I bring near My righteousness; it is not far off, and My salvation will not delay; I will put salvation in Zion, for Israel My glory."*

> (Isaiah 46:9-13)

Omnipotence also speaks of sovereignty and God is sovereign because He is the King. However, unlike our Queen who is a constitutional monarch here in the United Kingdom, God not only *reigns*, He also *rules* over all in all. These two facts, when combined, are potent. Consider, then, the nature of a gift without reservation from the hand of an omniscient and omnipotent God. What type of gift might we expect from Him?

> *"For the wages of sin is death, but the **free gift** of God is eternal life in Christ Jesus our Lord."* (Romans 6:23)

> *"For the **gifts** and the **calling** of God are **irrevocable**."*
> (Romans 11:29)

Repentance (*metanoia*) always speaks of a change of mind, a final sense of thought, judgement or *resolve*.

Traditionally, we have tended to associate the irrevocable nature of God's gifts with Charismatic endowments and we have used Romans 11:29 to reconcile what, to many, is irreconcilable, i.e., God not withdrawing His gifts from people or, more specifically, from ministries which we deem as no longer meriting His giftedness.

It is remarkable indeed that we should be prepared to extend this logic of grace to gifts of service and yet are unable to apply the same logic to the gift of God, i.e. salvation.

Having purposed to save us, God's saving resolve means that He will never change His mind concerning our position and He has further ensured this by making His gifts and calling *irrevocable*. Simply put, this means that we could not give back the gift of God even if we no longer want it.

If you say that you can lose your salvation, you are saying that you can revoke what God has said is irrevocable. Therefore, since God is omnipotent (i.e., all powerful), for you to say that you can walk away from salvation is to say that you are more powerful than God.

The Work of the Trinity

1. The Father

Our salvation was conceived in the heart of God from eternity past. The Architect of the universe is also the Architect of our salvation. Moreover, God's plan of salvation was executed even before the creation of the world and it was executed *for* us and not by us. Salvation is based not on what we are doing but on what God has done before the foundation of the world (Ephesians 1:3-7). God is committed to completing the work which He has begun in our lives (Philippians 1:6).

2. The Son

Jesus died for all of our sins, past, present and future, and now He is before the Father, interceding on our behalf (Hebrews 7:25). He is our Advocate (1 John 2:1). An advocate speaks of one who is alongside us; someone who is a defence lawyer. As our Advocate, Jesus does not protest our innocence, but rather He admits our guilt and confirms His sacrifice.

In addition, He is also our Judge and thus, for Christians to lose their salvation, Jesus (who is both our Defence Lawyer and our Judge) would have to stand before the Father and say, "I am sorry, I failed. I was the Advocate and the Judge, but I lost the case." That, surely, is to strain credibility (*cf.* John 6:37-40; John 10:27).

3. The Holy Spirit

The Holy Spirit seals (Ephesians 1:13-14) and He renews (Titus 3:5; 1 Peter 1:23). In the ancient world, the seal signified the end of a transaction, a mark of ownership or complete security. The Apostle Paul teaches us in Ephesians that the Holy Spirit is given as a *deposit* or *seal*. For us to lose our salvation means that the One who has paid for us will lose His deposit. Thus, the implication is clear. For us to be lost would mean that the Holy Spirit (our Deposit) would also be lost to the Godhead. That would be an unlikely proposition.

The Family of God

God is Love. One's status as a child does not change just because one might behave in a manner not pleasing to one's parents. Regardless of what we do, we remain children and likewise with the family of God. Nothing I can do can change the fact that my father is my father; even orphans, although not knowing their father, are still the father's children.

My salvation is secure because I belong to the family of God.

For us to lose the free gift of life, the unimaginable would have to happen. Jesus would have to stand up in heaven one day and say the following:

"I know I said that ..." + "The Jesus Problem"

You are justified – completely forgiven and made righteous.

But I was wrong.

You are saved and set apart according to God's grace.

I was wrong.

You have been redeemed through the cleansing Blood and forgiven of all your sins and the debt against you has been cancelled.

I have gotten it wrong. There is still an outstanding debt and I do not have wherewithal to pay it.

You have died with Christ and died to the power of sin's rule over your life.

Even though you died with Me, sin still has its hold over you.

You are free forever from condemnation.

I got it wrong. That is not what My Father in heaven meant. I apologize if I have ever given you reason to trust Him.

I have given you the Holy Spirit as a pledge, guaranteeing your inheritance.

I have lost my Deposit.

You have been chosen in Christ before the foundation of the world to be holy and you are without blame before Him.

Sorry, my sons and daughters, you have been deselected.

You have been predestined (i.e., determined by God) to be adopted as God's child.

You have never been adopted, only fostered.

I could go on and on with this ridiculous charade but I have made my point. God is not a man that he should lie. None of these things will ever happen to us because, my beloved, we are Safe and Sound.

"Now to Him who is able to keep you from stumbling and to present you blameless before the presence of His glory with great joy, to the only God, our Saviour, through Jesus Christ our Lord, be glory, majesty, dominion, and authority, before all time and now and for ever. Amen."

(Jude 24-25)

Of course, cynics would say that only fairy stories would begin with "Once upon a time" and end with "and they all lived happily ever after". I am happy to accept that statement. But I would definitely prefer my fairy story to the horror story of the religionists.

My journey began on the traumatic day when I discovered that I was a foster child. It was as though everything in my life had been a dreadful lie. I found it difficult to trust anyone. By the age of ten, the age of innocence was over for me. It was the survival of the fittest. Abandoned in an orphanage, terrified, confused and alone, I had to develop strategies to make life work. I had, in the words of the song, cried me a river. However, I have come to an unassailable truth – this little orphan boy is not an orphan anymore. There is One who loves me and that One has adopted me and thus, come what may, I can say, *"For I have not received the spirit of slavery to fall back into fear but I have received the Spirit of adoption as His son, by whom I cry, 'Abba! Father!'"* (Romans 8:15) and,

"The Lord Himself has redeemed me from being under the Law so that I might receive adoption as His son" (Galatians 4:5).

I can rejoice with the Apostle Paul and say, "Blessed be the God and Father of my Lord Jesus Christ, who has blessed me in Christ with every spiritual blessing in the heavenly places, even as He chose me, Paul Anderson-Walsh, in Him before the foundation of the world, that I should be holy and blameless before Him. *In love He predestined Paul Anderson-Walsh for adoption through Jesus Christ, according to the purpose of His will,* to the praise of His glorious grace, with which He has blessed us in the Beloved. In Him, Paul Anderson-Walsh has redemption through His blood, the forgiveness of trespasses, according to the riches of His grace, which He lavished upon Paul Anderson-Walsh, in all wisdom and insight making known to Paul Anderson-Walsh the mystery of His will, according to His purpose, which He set forth in Christ as a plan for the fullness of time, to unite all things in Him, things in heaven and things on earth. In Him, Paul Anderson-Walsh has obtained an inheritance, having been predestined according to the purpose of Him who works all things according to the counsel of His will, so that Paul Anderson-Walsh who was the first to hope in Christ might be to the praise of His glory. In Him, I also, when I heard the word of truth, the gospel of my salvation, and believed in Him, was sealed with the promised Holy Spirit, who is the guarantee of my inheritance until I acquire possession of it, to the praise of His glory."

Why not re-read the above passage from Ephesians 1 and replace my name with your name and you too will see that no matter what your "Once upon a time" might have been, you too will live happily ever after – safe in the knowledge that you can no more lose your salvation than you can earn it.

"I have no greater joy than to hear that my children are walking in the truth."

(3 John 4)

CHAPTER 34

EPILOGUE – LIFE AFTER
THE CREDIT CRUNCH

As I write this second edition in London in the Spring of 2009, the world is in the grip of a recession. The expression coined to describe this global predicament is the "credit crunch". As I reflect on this financial turmoil and the Child Phase of the Christian life, the "credit crunch" seems to me an apt metaphor for those of us who set out on our spiritual journeys.

The word "credit" is derived from the Latin word *creditum*, from *credere* which means to "believe" or "trust". As we have observed, belief and trust are the cornerstones of the Christian life. To move from where we are to where we have been called to go, each of us must come face-to-face with the crunch question – do we trust God? It is one part of faith to believe *in* God but quite another to *believe God*, i.e., to believe that He is in fact who the Bible says He is, that He has forgiven all of our sins and that He is nothing other than love and loving.

As we have witnessed in the global economy, when trust is broken, the market atrophies. Lenders and suppliers withdraw the facilities which make it possible for people to obtain goods or services before payment because credit is based on the trust that payment will be made in the future. When we refuse to trust

God the ramifications are serious. We too become guarded about extending ourselves to Him.

I hope that in this first volume of the trilogy, I have been able to persuade you that because of who God is, you and I are safe as sons and daughters because we have been adopted. In this Child Phase volume we have considered the idea of adoption through a Western lens and applied it to a displaced orphan. It is a vivid and vital image for us regarding salvation. However, as we prepare to put away these child-things and embrace the more mature truths, we will see the other side of the adoption coin, *viz.* being adopted carries the idea of being adapted.

As the Apostle Paul wrote in his letter to the church in Ephesus –

> *"For we are His workmanship, created in Christ Jesus for good works, which God prepared beforehand, that we should walk in them."*
>
> (Ephesians 2:10)

God has prepared works for us to do; all that remains is for Him to prepare us to do the works. And that, dear reader, is where we are headed for in this trilogy series. It is one thing for you to entrust to God what you care for, but it is quite another for God to entrust to you the things He cares for. And that is our destiny – to be the caretakers of all that is God's. To fulfil that destiny, we must be made *safe sons*. For us to participate in the good works prepared for us before the foundation of time, we must first discover what it means to be a son.

Once we grasp this revelation we, as the sons of God, must be brought to maturity through the Teenage Phase. A teenager comes into the fullness of his identity, exercises his authority that has been delegated to him, manages the heavenly resources that are at his disposal and becomes a reproducer of the life of Christ that is within him. The young teenager must grapple with bigger questions. Instead of wondering "Who am I in Christ?", he poses a more dangerous question, "Why is Christ in me?" And when, at length, his revelatory "Ah!" moment arrives, he sees it for what it is – Christ is in him not to translate him from earth to heaven (as he has at first supposed) but rather, to journey with him in transforming earth into heaven! As an adopted son, he sees that he is not simply a divine possession but is, in fact, possessed by the Divine. He is, if you will, part of *de*-vine. The Teenager is more than a conduit, container, passage, pipe or tunnel through which Christ's life passes. He realizes that God's *agapé* nature is defused through his whole being – mind, body, heart and soul – and is expressed uniquely in him through his personality. He now sees himself in the light, i.e., as an expresser of God's *agapé* nature, and as he lives his life, he coincidently makes God manifest.

So, as I sign off this first volume, when we next sit down for a chat in volume two, it will be for your induction into High School. In the meantime, enjoy the holidays and remember that it is through us, the Church, that God makes Himself known. We stand as proof of His existence. It is we who reveal His presence and make His appearance. We are those who are His manifestation. We are Him materialized. It is for good reasons that the Apostle Paul wrote in 2 Corinthians 5:17-21,

"Therefore, if anyone is in Christ, he is a new creation. The old has passed away; behold, the new has come. All this is from God, who through Christ reconciled us to Himself and gave us the ministry of reconciliation; that is, in Christ God was reconciling the world to Himself, not counting their trespasses against them, and entrusting to us the message of reconciliation. Therefore, we are ambassadors for Christ, God making His appeal through us. We implore [not "deplore"] you on behalf of Christ, be reconciled to God. For our sake He made Him to be sin who knew no sin, so that in Him we might become the righteousness of God."

Refrain from dispensing with this little book too soon. Make sure you have rooted these truths deep within you.

Imagine the wonder in store for us as we contemplate the implications of the fact that you and I are Ambassadors for Christ. We are the high-ranking diplomats accredited as representatives from the Kingdom of Heaven. Reflect, if you will, on the staggering fact that God is making His appeal through us and that He is drawing on us to call the world to His side, to console the world and to be the source of encouragement, strength, consolation and comfort.

There remains one truly recession-proof company on this earth. She has been sleeping for many years, but now I sense that she is being re-purposed and is returning to her core activity. You may know her as the Church. But I would like to re-brand her for our purposes: Jes-US, Sons & Daughters Unlimited. It will be a global operation with "branches" in every country in the world who will bear fruit for the healing of the nations.

See you next term!

Agapé,

Paul.

For more information about resources available from this author, visit www.paulanderson-walsh.com

---

We hope you enjoyed reading this New Wine book.
For details of other New Wine books
and a wide range of titles from other
Word and Spirit publishers visit our website:
www.newwineministries.co.uk
or e mail us on newwine@xalt.co.uk